STAFF 1946–PRESENT continued•Eric J. Downie•Howard Downing•Patrick Downing•Jackie Dowse•Kenneth C. Doyle•Ted Drauschak•Susan E. Drey•Paul Drumsta•Lelanya Drury•Andres Duany•Raisa Dubensky•Ernest J. Duberry Jr•Faustino R. Ducut•Carole Dudley•Erica S. Dudrow•Matthew Duerksen•Randy Duffy•Raymond M. Dufresne•Daniel Dugas•Larry Duggan•Theresa Dukes•Pamela Dull•Vytas Dulys•Carole Lynn Duncan•Terrell Duncan Jr•Lisa K. Dunkin•Carolyn Dunmyer•Fred P. Dunn•Michael Dunn•Rebecca Dunn•Robyn Dunn•Stephen Dunn•Tien Mank Duong•Lori A. Duperon•Erma Dupont•Lawrence Dupont•Anna Durant Ecker•Joseph John Duschl•Deborah Dutton•Neil Todd Duvernay•Royce M. Earnest•Steve Eastwood•Osamu Ebata•Richard A. Eberhardt•Pete Ebersole•Thomas Eckhardt•Arthur Eckhoff•Timothy Eddy•Carl S. Ede•Paul Edmeades•Sharon Efraimson•Dorothy L. Eggers•Adam Ehart•Christian Ehrman•Beverly Eichenlaub•Gina M. Eichensehr•Virginia Eichorn•Margaret Eiford•Bernard J. Eischen•Donna Eisenmann•Marie Eisman•Dorothy Elder•Thomas L. Eline•Ty Ellingson•Simon M.H. Elliot•Sue Elliott•Tim Elliott•Christopher Eelis•Joseph Ellis•Stephanie J. Ellis•Wayne Ellmon•Elizabeth R. Emerson•E. Kathy Emmons•Stephen Empie•Brita W. Engelke•Meggan W. Engelke•Jeffrey Engelskirch•Cathy Ann Engle•Paula Englehart•M. Eileen English•Terri P. Ennis•Richard Episcopo•H.A. Erauw•Wayne Ericksen•Vito Eringis•Juanda M. Escoe•Richard Esterle•Teresa Evanko•Diane Evans•Michael Evans•George Everding•Kevin Eyen•Carole L. Eyring•Tracy Ezell•Marcus W. Fairbrother•George Fambro•Chor-Man Fan•Xiaoming Fan•Ildefonso Fantone•O.D. Farinholt•Carol Farley•Mary Lee Farmer•Annabel V. Farrales•Stephen Farris•Dorsey Fast•Heather B. Faucher•Thomas Faucher•Lewis L. Faulkner•Jeffrey Faw•Wendy Fearing•David Feeback•James Feldman•Alexis Felix•Janet Felsten•Barbara A. Fennell•Ronald L. Ference•Chip Ferguson•Edward Ferguson•Herbert Ferguson•Michael Ferguson•Kay H. Fernandez•Margarita M. Fernandez•Zandra J. Fernandez•Marta H. Ferreira•C. David Feske•Stacey Fesler•Marc Fetterman•Wayne Feuerborn•Frances Fidler•Joel Fidler•Darell Fields•Jeanette Fiengo•John Filkins•Peter A. Fillat III•Michael A. Filler•M.H. Finch•Jeffrey A. Fineman•Scott Finfrock•Jerry Fink•Thomas Fink•Elizabeth Firth•Paul A. Firth•Fred Fishback•Nina Fishbeyn•David R. Fisher•Coy Fite•Annette Fitzgerald•John Fitzgerald•Mark Fitzgerald•Laura Fitzmaurice•W. Knox Fitzpatrick•David Fleeger•Monica R. Fleischman•Ilya Fleishman•Lynn Flemming•James Fletcher•Dorothy Flikier•Olegario R. Florendo•Sandra Floyd•Scott Foerst•Catherine Foertsch•John Foley•Thomas Follett•Kiat Foo•Laquita M. Ford•Robert Ford•Shirley Witherspoon Ford•Marilyn Forester•Jason D. Forney•Linda Forsythe•Holly L. Forusz•Lena Fosaas•Ann Fosnight•Jarmel L. Foster•John Foster•Pamela J. Fountain•Terry Fountain•Robert Fouse•Gregory L. Fowler•Kory M. Fox•Melody Fox•Roberta Fox•Harley Fran•Lenore Francisco•Irene Frankel•Jeanne Franklin•Ray Fraser•Paula M. Frauenknecht•Brian P. Fredley•Nathan Freebury•Daniel Freed•Dana French•Jennifer Freund•Carol Frey•Kenneth H. Friedlein•Brian Friedley•Carol Friedman•Lea Friedman•Louis Friend•Kurt Frimodig•Robert Fritzsche•Jennifer Frost•Russell O. Fuchs•Laurie Fuld•Felicity Fullford•Don Fulton•Steven Funk•Jeffrey N. Funke•Edward Funkhouser•Paul Furia•Hope Furrer•Dwayne G. Furukawa•William Gabriel•Amy L. Gaddis•Carol Gaetano•Dennis Gaffney•Theodore Gaffney•Samir J. Gaglani•Randolph D. Galang•Stephen L. Galbreath•Elizabeth Gallagher•John R. Gallagher•Carlos A. Gallego•Jon C. Gambrill•Jake (Jagdish) Gami•Daniel K. Gamor•Piter Gan•Frank Gant•Joann Ganwald•Xavier Garaud•Antonio Garcia•Joseph Garcia•Maria Garcia•Olga Garcia•Cristina Garcia-Lavin•Julio C. Garciafigueroa•Sheryl Garnecki•Allan Garner•Mary Garofalo•James Garretson•Earle Gartrell•Kenneth Garvin•Wesley Garwood•Lonnie Gary•Gintautos Gaska•Randal Gaskins•Suthichai Gasrapong•Catherine A. Gately•Michele Gatzmeyer•Vincent Gavin•Bret C. Gean•Delia Gebhart•Timothy G. Geddie•James R. Geiger•Walter Geiger•James Geigu•Howard Geisler•Angelo Gelsomino•Gregory Gensler•Michael C. Gentemann•Pam Gentilucci•Paul Gentner•Maria Georgiou•Gioia Gerard•Charles Gerlach•Sharon Gershowitz•Louis F. Geschwindner•David Gestor•Chester Gettys•Gregory Geusler•Nancy Giammatteo•Andrew Giba•Dawn E. Gibeck•Cristine C. Gibson•Emma H. Gibson-Smith•Peter Giddens•Kathryn A. Giebenhain•Antonio R. Giglio•Gordon Gilbert•Kenneth C. Gilbert•Timothy Gilbert•Franklin Giles•Pamela Gillen•William Gillett•Philip Gillette•Stephen Gilliss•Robert A. Gilp•Alan Gin•Gerard V. Gioia•John Gissendanner•Igor Givotovsky•Zoe A. Gizara•Philip Gladden•Beth Glasser•Geoffrey Glazer•Thomas Gleason•Donna J. Globus•Steven Glock•Marcus Glover•Erin B. Glynn•Gordon M. Godat•Rita Ann Godfrey•Katherine Godine•Richard Godwin•Mark Goeller•G. Ronald Goetz•Sharon Goetz•Norman Goldberg•Nancy Golder•David Goldrick•Dennis R. Goldrick•Sandra Goldschmidt•Ismail Gomaa•Cynthia D. Gongon•Manuel J. Gonzales•Corrine A. Gonzalez•Francisco Gonzalez•Gregory Good•Todd Goodale•Jane Goode•Mark Goodrich•Cherrie L. Goolsby•Maryann Gopar•Eric Gordon•Gary Gordon•Gerry Gordon•Elliot Gorstan•Cassandra Gottlieb•R. Michael Gotwald•Margaret E. Gowan•Cindy Gower•William Grabowski•Sharon Graeber•James Graham•Jay Graham•Leisa Graham•Marianne M. Graham•Sandra Graham•W. Barry Graham•Jason Neil Gramke•Rachel Grant•William Grape•Vicki Grasanti•Mark Grasmehr•Marc Graves•Thomas Graves•Edward L. Gray•Jerome Gray•Anthony Greco•Victor Greco•Merideth Greeber•Anita Green•Cynthia A. Green•Heather Green•Lynette Green•Marshall Green•Morris Green•William L. Green•Nancy Green-Schieken•Sebastian Greenall•Charles Greenawalt•Susan Greenberg•Kelley R. Greene•Kimberly Greene•Charles R. Greenland Jr•Joanne Greenwald•Michael P. Gregg•Janey Gregory•Thomas Gregory•Greg Gresham•Eric A. Gribble•Mark Gribbons•James R. Grieves•Christopher Griffin•Julia Griffin•Susan Griffith•Barbara L. Grimsley•Richard Grogan•Steven L. Grogg•Randall Groh•Katherine Grootendorst•Barbara Grossman•Charles Grote•Virginia Grote•Carol Grounds•Ronald Grubbs•Elwood Gruber•Meredith A. Gruber•Linda Guckert•Thomas Guerin•Ernest M. Guidry•Terry Guilbeau•Rajesh Gulati•Diane Guljas•Yigit Guloksuz•Jeffrey J. Gundel•Andrea M. Gunn•Kharma A. Gunn•M. Christina Gurucharri•Rolf Haarstad•Mohamed Habeeb•Elizabeth Hackbarth•Jennifer A. Haddaway•Catherine Hader•Timothy Haggerty•Kurt Haglund•Richard Hagy•Judith Hahn•Russ Hale•Margaret Haley•Catherine D. Hall•J.D. Hall•Kim S. Hall•Philip Hall•Samuel Hall•Stephen G. Hall•Trudy Hall•Parker Hallam•Craig Hallinshead•Patricia Hamilton•Kathy Hamlet•Kathleen Hammer•Patrick Hammers•Bradley R. Hammond•Cynthia Hammond•David Hammond•Barbara Hanba•Kenneth H. Hancock•Jeffrey Hancox•Barry Hand•Todd Haner•John D. Hansell•Jane Hansen•Mark Hansen•Silke Hansen•Michael J. Hanson•Dana Harbaugh•Melissa A. Harding•Scott Harding•Ray Hariri•Pamela Harloam•Brian Harper•Sylvia Harper•Arnetha T. Harriday•Lisa M. Harrigan•Christine Harrington•Robert L. Harris•George Harrison•James D. Harrison•Mary Harrison•Paul Harry•David Hart•John Hart•Kenneth A. Hart•Ronald J. Hartman•Harold Harvey•Erin C. Harwood•George Hascup•Mark Hasslinger•Ramin Hatef•Cynthia Hatfield•Jeffrey Hatfield•David Hathway•Patrick Hauck•David Hauk•Steven C. Hauk•Harvey C. Havland Jr•Steven Hawk•Edith Hawthorne•Charles Hax•Ronnell Hayden•Mary Hayes•Xiaojian He•Paul Head•Karen Joy Healy•Trisha M. Healy•Laura Hearns•Kimberly S. Heartwell•Mark Heatley•Gerald Heibe•Frederick Heidel•Pamela Heil•Wayne Heil•Tom Heineman•James K. Heinly•Kenneth N. Heit•Jo Anne Helman•D. Rodman Henderer•Gregory Henderson•Bruce S. Hendler•Carolyn Henger•Jerome F. Henger Jr•David Herbert•Robin Herrell•Antoni Herrero•Travis D. Herring•Janet Herschel•Deborah Hershowitz•Sandra Hersh•Hans Herst•Bryan Hethcoat•Kurt Heyssel•Lynn Hickey•Anne Hicks•Edward Hicks•Michael Hiett•Mark Hilderbrandt•Nels Hildeton•Jack Hileman•Jacqueline Hill•Jenifer Hill•Melanie Hill•Pamela C. Hill•Teruo Hina•Lou-Ann Hines•Kerry Hinton•Thomas Hippman•George W. Hirsch Jr•Karl D. Hirschmann•Frederick Hiser•Adela C. Ho•Harry Hochman•John Hochwalt•Helene V. Hodge•Jean Hodge•Diane Hodges•Elizabeth Hodgson•Kirk Hodulik•Ricardo Hoegg•Bonnie R. Hoerner•Charles Hoffman•Thomas Hoffman•Lisa Hogan•Michele Hogan•Judy Hohn•Dianna Holden•Virginia Holden•Ahna Holder•Charles Holifield•Tom Holifield•Ray Holliday•Craig Hollinshead•Larry Holman•Kristi Holmboe•D. Holmes•Mary Holmes•Michael L. Holmes•W.P. Holmes•Ann Holubec•James T. Hood•Janet L. Hook•Lisa A. Hopkins•Robert Hopkins•Richard Hopwood•Brian L. Horn•Kevin N. Horn•Christopher A. Hornbaker•Heather Horter•Bradfield R. Horton•Cheryl Horton•Newlyn Hosea•Jeffrey C. Hoskin•Jim Hossbach•Angela Houg•Thomas Houg•Eugene House•James House•William Houston•Tammy L. Houtz•Denita Howard•Janet Howard•Allen C. Howe II•Lewis Howie•David Hrdlicka•Konrad D. Hrehorowicz•Hui-Wen Hsiao•Charles C. Hsu•Liang-Lun Hu•Joanne Huang•Deborah Hubbard•Karl Erick Huber•Laura R. Huber•Neal Hudson•Lee Hughart•Barry S. Hughes•Ena C. Hughes•Michael Hughes•R.C. Hughes•Thomas P. Hughes•Barry Huhn•Canny Hui•Sarah Huie•John Hull•Stephen C. Hundley•Ching Hung•Chung-Ming Hung•Emily Y. Hung•Shirley S. Hung•Ron Hunot•Alison Hunt•James Hunt•Christopher Hunter•Dana Hunter•Joe L. Hunter•Richard Hurdle•Jacquelyn Hurt•Gail Hurwitz•Kevin Huse•Zulkifli Husin•Rahena R. Hussain•John D. Hutch III•Tim Hutcheson•Helen Hutchinson•Carl Hutzler•Carl Hyman•Michele Iacobucci•Stephen S. Iandolo•Rolando Idases•Nizar Idrisi•Masayuki Ikariya•Martin Illingworth•Robert Imperatrice•Nester Infanzon•Donna M. Irwin•Kirk Irwin•Karl Issacs•Nazree M. Ismail•Janice Izenberg•William T. Jack•Gregory S. Jackson•John Jackson•Kathy Jackson•Linda Jackson•Rhonda Jackson•William Jackson•Donald Jacobs•Jeffrey Jacobs•Philip Jaffarian•Martin Jafter•Stephen Jaklitsch•Ed Jakmauh•Greg Jakse•Anthony E. James•Barry R. James•Lloyd James•N.E. James•Tviet James•Ali Jannati•Martin J. Janousek•Richard F. [obscured] Jerome J. Jaworski•Parthiban Jayaraman•Jamie L. Jaye•Mary S. Jaye•Richard Jaymes•Allen Jayne•Youp Jeagal•Helen B. Jeff[obscured]reys•Jumana Jeha•(Jay) John Jenkins•Elbert Jenkins•Mark E. Jenkins•Kimberly J. Jennings•Leonard V. Je[obscured]nnette Johantgen•Michael Johncock•D.C. Johns•Bert L. Johnson•Christopher Johnson•Claire J. Johnson•Clar[obscured]son•Eric Johnson•Frederick M. Johnson•Jamie M. Johnson•Kristian Johnson•Larry Johnson•Lucy Johnson•[obscured]chard Johnson•Robert W. Johnson•Rodney A. Johnson•Steven Johnson•Katherine P Johnson-Sprague•Kimber[obscured]istopher Jones•Courtney L. Jones•D.C. Jones•Ellis Jones•Forest Jones•George W. Jones•Larry Jones•Pamela J. Jone[obscured]ordan•Philip Jordan•Arne Jorgensen•Ernesto T. José•Mervyn P. Joseph•Martin Josie•Norman Joyner•John Ju[obscured]M. Juneau•Paul Jung•Yasmin Jung•Charlie Jung-Tsu Tai•Lisa Justus•Allen Kachel•Eric Kachile•Judith Kachilla•[obscured]rd R. Kagan•Margaret Kahal•Michael P. Kaiser•Robert W. Kaiser•Todd B. Kale•Shari L. Kallmyer•Seema K. Kalothia•Thom[obscured]Edward C. Kane•Ziad Kanaan•Ann Kaplan•Robert Kaplan•Iris Karcher•Peter Karol•Robert J. Karp•Gen Kato•Jonathan Kathel•Ellen Katz•Sally Katz•Deborah Kausch•Patricia A. Kazinski•Phyllis Kearns•Bobby Keaton•Sally Keech•Joe N. Keeton•Richard Keist•Brian Keith•Catherine D. Kellam•Kathryn Kelley•Janet Kelly•Posey Kelly•Steven C. Kelso•Daniel Kemme•Suzanne Kemp•Steven T. Kenat•Martha Kendrick•Russell E. Kennedy•Jeffrey Kennelly•Alan Kenney•Kimberly Kenney•Anita Kercheval•Robert Keremes•Patricia G. Kerulis•James M. Kettler•Naomi M.L. Kettler•Meng Kho•Rabih Khoury•Harley Kilborn•James S. Kilbourn•Ian Kiloh•Choo Kim•Kwang B. Kim•Mi-Hwan Kim•Sun Chang Kim•Theresa M. Kim•Young Lib Kim•David Kimball•James Kimball•Don Kindsvatter•Perserphone King•Richard P. King•John Kinnaird•Allen Kinney•Yoko Kinoshita•Alan Kirk•Scott Kirk•William Kirk•Michael J. Kirkpatrick•Thomas Kirvan•James R. Kitko Jr•Romano Klepec•Matthew S. Klinzing•Nicholas G. Klise•Thomas F. Klose•Julie A. Klump•Thomas Kneeshaw•Robert Knight•Andrea D. Knisley•Edwin Knowles•Glenn Knowles•Timothy E. Knudsen•Karl Knutsen•Karen S. Koenig Blose•David Kofahl•Kimberlee Kofsky•Y.C. Eric Koh•Kimberly Kohlhaas•Charles L. Kokoski•Gretchen Kolakoglu•M. Brian Kolar•James Kolker•Christine Kondner•Wayne Kookogey•Sherrie Kormann•Alex Kosich•Demetri P. Koutrouvelis•Oscar Kovarrubias•Sherrie Kovmann•Thomas M. Kowalski•Gregory Kozak•Jerome S. Kozak•Masashi Kozima•Kathy Kramer•Jay Kratz•Dan-Michael Krisher•Mark R. Kroeckel•Elaine Kropueld•Sandra Kroth•Sharon A. Kroupa•Jackie Krueger•Michael P. Kruger•J, Mark Krukiel•Kelsey A. Kruse•Mark Ksiazewski•Jill Kurfirst•Douglas Kuriga•Anne Kurtz•Ralph H. Kurtz•Howard Kurushima•Earl Randolph Kuser•Robert Kutner•Linda E. Kyle•Johanna La Pierre•Renato S. Lacson•Paul J. Ladensack•Troylene Ladner•

THE MASTER ARCHITECT SERIES II

RTKL

Selected and Current Works

First published in Australia in 1996 by
The Images Publishing Group Pty Ltd
ACN 059 734 431
6 Bastow Place, Mulgrave, Victoria, 3170
Telephone (61 3) 9561 5544 Facsimile (61 3) 9561 4860

National Library of Australia Cataloguing-in-Publication Data

    RTKL.
       RTKL: selected and current works.

       Bibliography.
       Includes Index.
       ISBN 1 875498 53 2.
       Master Architect Series II ISSN 1320 7253

       1. RTKL. 2. Architecture, American.
       3. Architecture, Modern—20th century—United States.
       4. Architects—United States. I. Title.
       (Series: Master Architect Series II).

   720.92

Edited by Patricia Sellar

Co-ordination: Thom McKay and Jo Helman

Designed by Laurent Marrier d'Unienville for Blur Pty Ltd,
Mulgrave, Australia

Film separations by Scanagraphix Australia Pty Ltd

Printing by Everbest Printing, Hong Kong

Contents

INTRODUCTION

RTKL Founders:
Archibald C. Rogers, Francis T. Taliaferro, Charles E. Lamb, George E. Kostritsky

RTKL:
The First Fifty Years

By Larry Paul Fuller

P erusing the literature of architecture firm
management, one repeatedly encounters the
observation—expressed in various ways—that the
delivery of creative services is complicated by
opposing points of view: "How did that project
come out?" versus "How did we come out on that
project?". Those firms that achieve a balance
between the two concerns—aesthetic and
monetary— are said to be those who are most
likely to succeed.

Indeed, the enviable success of RTKL Associates—
consistently ranked among the top five or six
American AE firms in terms of annual billings,
yet also widely respected for its design—is often
attributed to the balance it achieves between
quality architecture and quality management.
While this general sentiment is true, "balance"
implies a kind of give-and-take—a compromise
between desired ends—that doesn't seem to fit at
RTKL, where there is not only an unbending
commitment to good management and corporate
profitability, but also a true passion for good
design. It is an ambitious, almost naive, we-can-
have-it-all notion that was expressed succinctly by
RTKL chairman Harold Adams almost 30 years
ago when, soon after being brought in to manage
the firm, he responded to potentially contentious
probing by his new colleagues. "Are we in this for
good *profits*, or good *design*?" came the question.
With no hint of compromise, Adams replied:
"We're in it for *both*."

And, here on the brink of its fiftieth year, RTKL
remains "in it" in a very big way. The 500-person
design firm is not only big, but also diversified,
multilocational, and multidisciplinary. The people
of RTKL represent a comprehensive menu of
disciplines, including: architecture, planning and
urban design, interior architecture, landscape
architecture, engineering, and environmental
graphic design. By project type, the firm's work
spans a spectrum including: retail, government,
mixed-use, health science, planning, interiors, hotel,
housing, office, graphics, and transportation.
The work also spans the globe; headquartered
in Baltimore, RTKL achieves a worldwide reach
through its expanding network of domestic offices
(also Dallas, Washington, Los Angeles) and three
offices overseas (London, Tokyo, Hong Kong),
as well as through strategic alliances in Mexico,
Germany, Australia, and China.

So to look back from the vantage point of RTKL's
golden anniversary is to trace the growth and
development of a firm that evolved through stages
of local, regional, and national prominence to its
present status as a truly global practice that
happens to be headquartered in America.

49 College Avenue, Annapolis, Maryland

Lamb, Taliaferro, and Rogers

The design studio

Girl Scout Lodge

Salvation Army Day Nursery

And throughout its evolution, RTKL has embraced the earliest ideals on which the firm was built, and by which it has prospered far beyond normal expectation.

HANGING OUT A SHINGLE

The earliest vestiges of RTKL go back to a grandmother's basement in Annapolis, Maryland, where Princeton graduate Archibald Rogers began practicing architecture in 1946. Moving quickly beyond the limits of a solo practice, he soon formed a partnership with Francis Taliaferro, a World War II Marine captain who had answered Rogers' advertisement for a draftsman. Busying themselves with remodelings, houses and small-scale buildings, the two were joined in 1949 by Charles Lamb, then still a student at the University of Michigan.

Among Lamb's first assignments at the fledgling firm was the design of a Lodge for the Girl Scouts of Anne Arundel County. On rare occasions the meaning of "design excellence" is made clear through a building whose form, function and symbolic content coalesce into a powerful statement. Such was the modest structure that established the design reputation of RTKL's founders—Rogers, Taliaferro and Lamb.

The elegantly simple lodge was applauded in the professional press and received a national AIA design award in 1954. It also served well as a catalyst for further acclaim: one of the members of the AIA jury happened to be M.I.T.'s Pietro Belluschi, who was so impressed with the lodge that he chose to associate with the young firm for the design of the Church of the Redeemer in Baltimore—which was also honored nationally—as well as for the Goucher College student center. Within its first decade, the small firm had achieved a critical mass of momentum that would eventually propel it into the realm of large-firm success.

COMPLEMENTARY STRENGTHS

If the weight of Charles Lamb's contribution to the firm was gifted design, the thrust of Frank Taliaferro's concerns related to client service, and Arch Rogers' focus was on urban planning. Even today, the core beliefs of RTKL are neatly symbolized by the respective professional strengths of these three founders. The passion for design quality lives on as the firm competes globally in the design marketplace, always pursuing the creative spark, interested in the art of architecture, but also the rightness of it, how it serves its purposes, how it fits, and how it maximizes client resources.

Harundale Mall

State Office Building, Annapolis

Church of the Redeemer

Goucher College Center

Riverton Pumping Station

John Deere Regional Warehouse

The perpetuation of Taliaferro's belief in impeccable client service has resulted in solid relationships and multiple commissions from prestigious clients such as IBM, Hyatt, Johns Hopkins, Federated Department Stores, and The Rouse Company.

Original founder Arch Rogers' interest in planning also remains, not only as a distinct discipline within the RTKL scope of services, but also as an influence on the way design is approached and evaluated. The firm's roots in planning create a big-picture mind-set that goes beyond buildings as isolated objects in space to consider how they fit in a broader context, how they work with other buildings. It is an influence that encourages the subordination of egos and tends to discourage monumental personal design statements.

By the late 1950s, Arch Rogers had gained a regional reputation as an eloquent spokesman on urban design issues and agreed to head the Baltimore business community's efforts to rebuild a deteriorating city core. This activity led to the Charles Center Redevelopment Plan, which in turn resulted in the firm's selection to provide urban design and architectural services for the public portions of the Charles Center. This very significant commission prompted the firm to relocate in downtown Baltimore. And it also occasioned the completion of the original foursome, the addition of the "K" in RTKL, Harvard professor and urban designer, George Kostritsky.

EARLY GROWING PAINS

Beyond key roles in the revitalization of downtown Baltimore, Kostritsky's early contributions included his recruitment of several future RTKL leaders, such as Ted Niederman, and George Pillorgé, a Kostritsky protégé at Harvard who joined the firm in 1964. (Following the precedent of his mentor, Pillorgé would not only assume major roles in firm management, urban design and other projects, but would also maintain firm ties to academia through periodic teaching stints, active recruitment at selected universities, and the establishment of substantial student internship and fellowship programs.)

The success of Charles Center would lead to planning commissions beyond Baltimore—notably Hartford, Cincinnati and Dallas, eventually over a dozen others in addition to masterplanning opportunities for such new-town communities as Montgomery Village near Washington, DC, and portions of Reston, Virginia. RTKL was well-positioned for subsequent architectural commissions in the Inner Harbor area, which ultimately included the firm's first hotel, a Hyatt;

St Timothy's School

The Office at Cross Keys

Corning Public Library

Charles Center

Johns Hopkins Hospital

Montgomery Village

nearly a dozen office buildings; a federal courthouse; and, later, the Charles Center metro station. (More recently, RTKL provided masterplanning and urban design services for the highly acclaimed Oriole Park at Camden Yards.)

While new commissions are the life blood of any practice, Rogers Taliaferro Kostritsky Lamb in the mid-1960s was an apparently thriving 40-person firm so overwhelmed with work that no one had the time or the inclination to manage the firm's business. What they needed was someone to provide the missing dimension of a managerial focus. That someone turned out to be a young understudy from John Carl Warnecke's office named Harold Adams, who was hired to manage the firm in 1967, and who as its current chairman is widely respected in architectural circles as the guru of large-firm management.

SURE HAND AT THE HELM

A product of small-town (Palmer) Texas, Adams earned his architecture degree at Texas A&M in 1962. After receiving an offer (but no start date) with I.M. Pei, he subsequently accepted a job with Warnecke on the Kennedys' Lafayette Square project in Washington. Adams' diplomatic success in smoothing out what had become a difficult project secured him a role as Warnecke's right arm in Washington, where he developed a personal rapport with the Kennedys themselves (meeting with President Kennedy to select the site for his presidential library and later serving as project manager for his tomb). In Warnecke's San Francisco office after Lafayette Square, Adams' privileged status continued and he proceeded to learn all the intricacies of running a firm.

Pursued intently by the founders of Rogers Taliaferro Kostritsky Lamb, and promised full authority to manage, Adams accepted the position of Managing Architect for the firm in 1967. Simultaneously, the practice was reorganized as a general business corporation, RTKL Associates Inc. The idea of four partners relinquishing individual power for the good of the organization was somewhat visionary, if also entirely consistent with the notion of a team orientation— subordination of egos to achieve a responsible, people-oriented architecture.

Under Adams' leadership, the firm grew in the 1970s and 1980s from a relatively large architectural firm with dozens of people to a true giant with multiple disciplines and a staff measured in hundreds.

Paramus Park

Cincinnati 2000

Fountain Square

Hyatt Regency Baltimore

Inner Harbor Center

RETAIL ARCHITECTURE AS FUEL FOR GROWTH

The catalyst for the dramatic growth that propelled RTKL from a regional presence into the national and international arenas was its well-timed and innovative entry into design for retail development. The firm's initial dabbling in retail began in the late 1950s with the design of developer James Rouse's first enclosed mall—Harundale Mall, near Baltimore—and a foothold was well established by the early 1970s with the design of his Paramus Park Mall in New Jersey. Principal Frank Taliaferro saw retail as an opportunity and—along with team members Joe Scalabrin and Gary Bowden—took the work seriously. It was the success of Paramus and this early affiliation with Rouse that marked the beginning of a major involvement in retail.

Drawing on its planning perspective, those fundamental notions of what gives a city its vitality, it was only natural for the firm to promote a broader range of experiences in retail settings— food courts, movie theaters, a prevailing sense of pageantry, even sheer entertainment. (It was also natural for the firm to segue gracefully into large-scale mixed-use developments in which retail would often serve as the economic engine for a broader range of uses, including office, hotel and even residential.)

The work at Paramus included a major department store for A&S, the first of many for that company and others. The whole process was much like the growth of a tree from a small seed. Eventually, although its roots remained in Baltimore, the firm would have to branch out in order to serve the demands of retail clients active in the Sun Belt, on the West Coast, and beyond.

STRENGTH THROUGH DIVERSIFICATION

In a firm committed not only to survival, but to prosperity, there are good arguments for diversification as a way to mitigate market uncertainties. Taking the strategy to its outer limits, RTKL has diversified by discipline, by building type, and also geographically. Of course the firm had started out with the discipline of planning as a service and also a sensibility, a special dimension to its architecture. As projects became more complex, and as one building type led to another, RTKL decided to add in-house engineering services. A structural engineering department was organized in 1971 and was followed by mechanical and electrical in 1975. Engineering has thrived at RTKL as a logical complement to architecture and the notion of full service. In the 1970s and 1980s, the firm added

Baltimore's inner harbor

Francis Scott Key Pavilion

Headquarters for Federated Department Stores

IBM, Manassas, Virginia

St Louis Center

interior design, landscape architecture and graphic design—a high-impact discipline extending from print work and architectural signing into the more exciting, quasi-architectural realm of environmental graphics.

MULTIPLE BUILDING TYPES

The development of multiple disciplines within the firm has been accompanied by, and partly driven by, diversification of building types. Some commissions have evolved naturally from previous projects and client relationships. Successful completion of the Hyatt Regency Baltimore, for example, has led to completion of more than a dozen other hotels, and a strong presence in hotel design. Other types of commissions have been the carefully calculated result of sophisticated marketing strategies. The firm became concerned a number of years ago, for example, that its percentage of retail and commercial work was too high. It pushed hard in both the governmental and health-care areas (the latter led by David R. Beard), which now account for a healthy 35 per cent of billings.

BEYOND BALTIMORE

When it came time to consider expanding beyond the Baltimore headquarters in the late 1970s, due primarily to pressure from a growing list of retail clients, there was considerable RTKL board meeting discussion about how best to establish new offices. One point of view favored buying out existing firms in the selected markets, a practical and expedient way to establish an immediate presence. But expedience lost out to judiciousness— a realization that it was important to transplant authentic components of the corporate culture in order to preserve it. The result is truly a single firm composed of several offices, rather than several firms tied together merely by accounting.

EXPANDING DOMESTICALLY

The first regional RTKL office was established in 1979 in Dallas, then an active market, by Joseph Scalabrin, who had been an influential architect with the firm since 1967 and (along with George Pillorgé and Harold Adams) was one of the key second-generation leaders. Under Scalabrin, assisted by David Brotman, the Dallas office weathered economic downturns and managed to grow steadily. Now directed by Lance Josal, the Dallas office is one of the largest in that city.

Canal Place

Boca Town Center

IBM Education Center at Thornwood

USF&G Mount Washington campus

Embassy of Singapore

Initially specializing in interior design, the Washington DC office was established in 1984 and now represents one of the largest architecture and interiors practices in Washington. It is well-positioned for government work and has gained particular notice for the Embassy work of Bernie Wulff and Rod Henderer.

Capitalizing on rapid growth in South Florida, a Fort Lauderdale office was opened in 1985 by Tom Gruber. After Fort Lauderdale came a long-sought West Coast presence established with the opening of the Los Angeles office in 1987. Now run by David Brotman, who had played a key role in the success of the Dallas office, L.A. was given its good start by principals Thomas Wheatley, Sudhakar Thakurdesai, and Paul Jacob.

GOING GLOBAL

As the regional offices became established, the Baltimore headquarters also grew and still houses about half of the firm's total staff. But by the time the RTKL network had been expanded to major United States centers, the trend toward a global economy had escalated. RTKL was already competing internationally in the mid-1980s, with projects in Australia, Brazil and Canada. But recognizing that the greatest market for its services into the next century may well be outside North America, RTKL began focusing on additional foreign opportunities. One of the biggest of those opportunities was at least partly serendipitous.

On a typical day at RTKL, in April of 1987, Harold Adams' mail contained a letter from a subsidiary of a Japanese firm previously unknown to RTKL. It was apparently a routine request for credentials and, as is customary, was handled promptly and with courtesy. Soon afterwards, RTKL was invited to meet with the prospective client in the Los Angeles office. What emerged from the meeting was an invitation to Tokyo and, equally important, a meeting of the minds—a good first impression that evolved into a relationship with one of Japan's largest corporations. In short order, RTKL became involved in several large projects for Japanese clients in Japan, throughout Southeast Asia, and in the United States.

RTKL's ties to Japan date to the 1960s when a cadre of Japanese graduate students from Harvard was invited to work in the firm's Baltimore office. The students benefited from an opportunity to study American architectural design and technology firsthand. And RTKL benefited by learning about Japanese culture and business practices. Building on these early ties, and riding the momentum of new client relationships and

Commerce Place

Baltimore office

Dallas office

Washington, DC office

Los Angeles office

significant projects, RTKL opened its Tokyo office, managed by Michitaka Yamaguchi, in 1990. (A strong sign of RTKL's acceptance in Japan was the 1993 registration of Harold Adams under the government's Strict B Criterion, signified by a prestigious "first class Kenchikushi" license.)

With the door to Japan ajar, other growth opportunities beckoned. A now-thriving and fully self-supporting London office, directed by Paul Hanegraaf, was also established in 1990. A Hong Kong office, currently led by Greg Yager, opened in 1994, positioning the firm for continued activity in the Pacific Rim. (Adams, Scalabrin and Brotman—who is the current vice chairman of RTKL—played leading roles in establishing these international outposts.) With its extensive resources and connections, RTKL will continue to maintain an opportunistic posture toward growth.

London office

Tokyo office

Hong Kong office

A LEGACY EXTENDED

With its original founders retired, its operating systems firmly established, and the grooming of third-generation leadership well under way, RTKL is poised for the future. Much has been written and said about the philosophy of RTKL, its managerial prowess, its rise to success. But what about that which ultimately matters most: its public legacy of city plans and buildings and spaces that bear its stamp?

There were the seminal buildings that established a reputation: the "teepee," the Church of the Redeemer and, in the late 1960s a warehouse for John Deere that— with its tension-cable roof, column-free space and minimalist forms—was both innovative and iconographically correct. The highlights of the 1970s included Cincinnati's Fountain Square, a triumph in consensus-building as well as urban design, and in that same city—late in the decade—there was the gleaming, pleated, triangular tower for Federated Department Stores that so forcefully broke out of the box. And work for IBM paved the way for more corporate commissions.

In the 1980s, financial success continued. The work got done and clients—many of them large-scale retail developers—were well served. (Cleveland's Tower City Center, one of the most ambitious urban development efforts ever undertaken in the United States, was begun and kept portions of RTKL's Dallas office busy for nearly ten years.) But there were voices within the firm calling for a stronger emphasis on design. Through a series of meetings at all levels of the firm in 1990, RTKL collectively developed and canonized a philosophy that emphasizes design first, followed by its clients, its people (who tend to stay with the firm once they get there), and its management. The firm also established a Design Forum of senior designers charged with developing tactics to sustain momentum in the area of design quality.

In a cluster of design achievements at the end of the 1980s and the beginning of the 1990s, there was the Marsh & McLennan building in Baltimore, a model of adaptive use involving an overtly modern, yet sympathetic, addition to a venerable cast-iron landmark. There was the Old San Juan Waterfront, in Puerto Rico, which received national urban design accolades as a sensitive redevelopment project. There was the intricately detailed Embassy of Singapore a deft reinterpretation of Singapore's vernacular building stock for the Washington climate. And, harkening back to the sheer force and clarity of the "teepee," there was the sculpture studio for the Maryland Institute, College of Art in Baltimore—a national-award-winning pro bono project that combined the practical suitability of a temporary work place with a temple-like spirit of tranquillity.

More recently, we've seen the completion of RTKL's 30-story Commerce Place office tower in Baltimore, three floors of which are occupied by the firm's headquarters. A lesson in contextualism, it defers politely to its surroundings through its classical three-part form and its richly detailed glass and masonry skin.

We've also seen the completion of the first phase of Reston Town Center, an "instant downtown" created as an eclectic mix of richly detailed buildings, plazas, fountains and pedestrian amenities—a well-defined core that offers the vitality of urban life within a rapidly developing suburban context.

INTERNATIONAL WORK SPAWNS
EXUBERANCE

If dramatic growth from retail commissions was the major influence of the 1960s, the most profound current influence at RTKL is the transition to a global practice. RTKL projects now span some 45 countries in Europe; North, South and Central America; Asia, particularly the Pacific Rim; the Middle East; and Australia. The firm's international billings have grown from one per cent of revenues to the current 35 per cent in just seven years, giving RTKL the second-largest non-United States market billings total in the world among international AE firms, according to recent *Engineering News-Record* rankings.

By contrast with domestic projects, some of the international work represents a dramatically larger scale—downtown mixed-use megablocks, a whole new town for Chinese tourists, and the world's tallest hotel, for example. The range of project types is also broader because of market demand in all the building categories, and because there tends to be less insistence by international clients on type-specific specialization. (How else could RTKL's office in Dallas—the antitheses of mass transit—be awarded a project like the Miyazaki train station in Japan?)

Perhaps the most gratifying aspect of going global, however, is the sheer exuberance—the freshness and vitality—that characterizes the firm's work as it responds to unfamiliar cultures and new design opportunities. There is The Manhattan hotel, for example, towering with poise over Tokyo Bay, deliberately Deco-esque, yet true to the Japanese aesthetic. There is the ever-so-exotic Tanjung Aru Resort, in east Malaysia, whose indigenous wood-frame construction seems to emerge from the lush landscape of its ocean-side setting. In Europe, the Amstel InterContinental hotel, of Amsterdam, epitomizes the artful renovation and expansion of a memory-filled old building. And on the boards, throughout RTKL, there is exciting work to come that reflects a global cross-pollination and a new momentum—creative energy to propel the firm into its second fifty years.

Larry Paul Fuller is a former editor of Texas Architect *magazine and a current principal in the Austin design and communication firm, Fuller Dyal & Stamper.*

SELECTED AND CURRENT WORKS

Retail

Northridge Fashion Center

Design/Completion 1991/1995
Northridge, California
MEPC American Properties Inc.
Steel and concrete
Interior stone finishes and granite floors

RTKL's extensive renovation of Northridge Fashion Center has repositioned the mall as one of the region's premier retail centers. With six major department stores and more than 200 specialty retailers and restaurants, Northridge Fashion Center now provides area shoppers with high-quality stores offering a wide variety of merchandise.

Along with extensive site improvements, landscaping and construction of four new parking decks, the renovation and expansion provide skylights, extensive interior landscaping, enhanced finishes and flooring, new elevators and escalators, and a new food court.

1

1   Center court
2   Entry from car park
3   Project identity graphics
4   Main retail corridor
5&6   Project identity graphics

2

3

4

5

6

The Courtyard Shops of Encino

Design/Completion 1991/1993
Encino, California
Security Pacific Corporation
100,000 square feet
Polished Italian granite, cement plaster and cast stone details;
perforated metal light sconces and custom wall medallions

The Courtyard Shops of Encino offer
residents of this California city a dramatic,
open-air environment for shopping,
dining, and other services.

In this elegant center courtyard shops are
efficiently arranged on three levels,
providing customers with easy access to a
wide array of high-quality fashions, gifts,
and housewares from around the world.
Over 30 specialty shops are available along
with restaurants offering both indoor and
outdoor dining.

Ample parking for nearly 500 cars further
enhances the convenience of the center
for local residents.

1

2

1   Central courtyard
2   Courtyard detail

Menlo Park

Design/Completion 1987/1991
Edison, New Jersey
The O'Connor Group
1.6 million square feet GLA
Steel
Brick and limestone cladding

Responding to the changing local market, RTKL transformed this existing one-level center into an upscale two-level retail mall and added a new 250,000-square-foot Nordstrom (not designed by RTKL) as a second anchor along with Macy's.

Although much of the existing 1970s structure was demolished, RTKL saved the foundation and a portion of the old mall. While the intention was to save time and cost, the approach required a precise design and uncompromising construction.

One major difficulty overcome was the fact that a part of the Macy's store was beneath the old mall that was to be demolished. The solution was a carefully engineered bracing system to support that portion of the center. The structure was then disassembled rather than demolished, allowing Macy's to remain open during the work.

The new mall's design is accented by marble flooring, custom-designed glass handrails with mahogany wood caps, brass light fixtures, geometric topiary, and other European-inspired landscaping.

1

2

1   Retail corridor
2   Staircase detail

Farmers Market

Design 1993
Los Angeles, California
Gilmore Company and JMB
700,000 square feet
Steel frame sheathed in metal panels and cement plaster
atop poured-in-place concrete

RTKL's addition to this historic open air regional mall is sensitive to the original structure from the 1930s, adding 25,000 square feet of retail space as well as two new anchor department stores.

The design attempts to break down the volume of spaces and facades while retaining the strength of a conservative and proven retail diagram. Landscaped courts, a primary feature of the design, act as transitional spaces between the new and existing areas and serve as major orienting spaces for shoppers and visitors. One such court contains a grand stairway and formal fountain, providing an area for community gatherings and small concerts.

Addressing the urban setting, the main facade is made up of covered arcades, awning-clad storefronts, and decorative paving, enhanced by fountains and outdoor furniture.

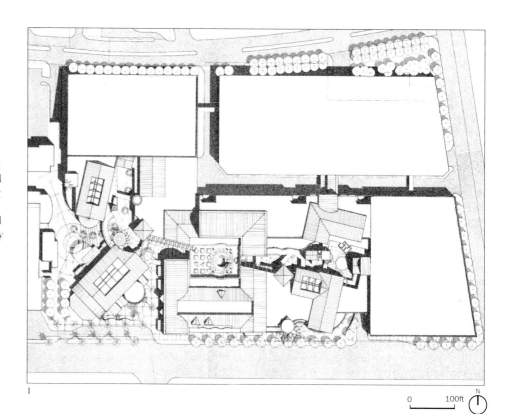

1

0   100ft

N

2

3

1   Roof plan
2   Building section
3   Building elevation

The Boulevard

Design/Completion 1989/1992
Las Vegas, Nevada
MEPC American Properties Inc.
215,000 square feet (refurbishment);
350,000 square feet (addition)
Concrete shell structure
Re-clad with perforated metal panels, glass and steel framework

Boulevard Mall, located in suburban Las Vegas, represents a significant trend in commercial development over the last decade—the expansion/renovation of existing retail centers. RTKL comprehensively refurbished this existing one-level mall and designed a new connecting addition.

The design objectives involved a major expansion that was visually compatible with the existing structure (much of which could not be altered or removed), a consolidation of the existing food tenants within a new food court, the improvement of existing site circulation and parking, while maintaining full operations during construction.

Adding variety and hierarchy to the two main malls, the design manipulates ceilings, walls, and floors so that the Promenade between the anchor stores becomes an enjoyable experience.

RTKL's graphics for the project included site signage, mall identity, directional signs, parking signs, food court imaging, and design.

1   Center Court
2   Door handle with graphic identity
3   Project signage
4   Refurbished entry with re-dressed columns

Farmers Market at Atrium Court

Design/Completion 1989/1990
Newport Beach, California
Irvine Retail Properties
Two-story steel frame construction on a poured-in-place concrete "table"
Exterior facade in metal panels and cement plaster

Challenged to create a new food venue for the successful Fashion Island property, RTKL converted an existing JC Penney department store into Farmers Market, an unusual dining environment in the Atrium Court building.

Farmers Market has a casual atmosphere with the sensory appeal of a European marketplace. Natural, hard-wearing materials, finishes, and unique furniture such as French bistro chairs add to the European flavor. Custom-designed maple banquettes and stand-ups define the edge of the seating area and provide alternate dining options.

A relaxed circulation path unlike those in many traditional food courts adds to the open-air feeling. Three-dimensional tenant storefront designs feature an eclectic and interesting mixture of materials from Raja slate to brushed stainless steel while the paving design incorporates French limestone, granite, and mosaic tiles.

RTKL also designed exterior and interior signage, directories, and escalator/elevator graphics.

1

1   Food court tenants
2   Central seating area
3&4   Food court tenants

2

3

4

Brandon Town Center

Design/Completion 1990/1995
Brandon, Florida
JMB Retail Properties Company
1,000,000 square feet
Brick facade with steel structure

This expansive one-level enclosed retail center east of Tampa is part of an overall plan that creates a lively retail core for the town of Brandon. The center contains over 350,000 square feet of GLA for specialty retail and restaurants.

With its red brick buildings, church steeples, and white-painted trim, Brandon has the look of a quiet northeastern community rather than a typical Florida town. Brandon Town Center continues this tradition with decorated red brick facades and five steeple-like towers (of five to seven stories each) that march through the full length of the center, announcing principal interior spaces and providing a strong exterior profile.

Inside, Brandon Town Center is characterized by lofty, vaulted malls and courts. A combination of roof skylights and clerestories floods the public areas with natural light while providing shade from

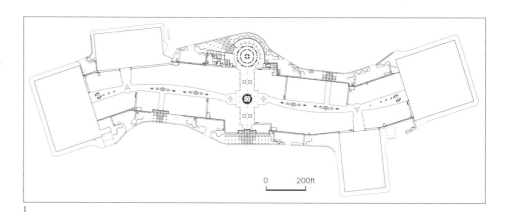

0   200ft

1

2

the relentless Florida sun. Major roof trusses and other structural elements have been deliberately exposed and brightly colored to provide visual excitement and a strong sense of order. Four towers identify intermediate courts; the fifth and tallest soars above the food court.

The center court's vaulted roof is two and one-half stories high with exposed steel trusses trimmed in bright colors to lend a playful aspect to the space. Directional and decorative graphic elements are based on some of Florida's most important indigenous wildlife. These "Critters," as the frogs, alligators, manatees, geckos, and pelicans are known, add a special charm. They appear on signs and structural elements and most notably, in the outstanding Tower Court sculptures by artist Jo Schneider.

4

3

5

Centro Augusta

Design/Completion 1993/1995
Zaragoza, Spain
SICIONE, S.A.
Associate Architects: José M. Gazoa and Fernando R. de Azúa
Interior design of a new 150,000-square-meter retail center
Concrete structure with brick work and pre-cast concrete panel cladding

Aimed at boosting the project's commercial viability and better responding to the leasing strategy established by the client, RTKL's commission for this new retail center in southern Spain began with an analysis of an existing design. Although construction had already started at the time RTKL was asked to become involved, slight modifications to the retail diagram achieved the client's financial goals without compromising the design intent established by the local architects.

Once this was established, RTKL provided interior design and graphic design services, creating an environment that was not only clean and contemporary but also alluded to the city's rich Augustan history and culture. Ceramic tiles, painted metal and glass combine to give the center a strong, sophisticated feel.

Centro Augusta boasts the largest Continente Hypermarket in Spain—15,000 square meters over two levels—as well as a nine-screen cinema and parking for 3,000 cars.

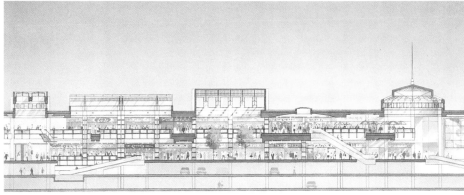

1

2

1   Central court
2   Section
3   Main atrium
4   Main retail corridor

3

4

Centro Oberhausen

Design/Completion 1990/1997
Oberhausen, Germany
Neue Mitte Projektentwicklung GmbH & Co. KG,
a subsidiary of the Stadium Group
Associate Architect: Architekten RKW
Concrete frame
Brick, masonry and glazed curtain wall

In the master plan by RTKL, Centro Oberhausen is distinguished by three major zones—the retail center, including the Oasis food court; the Promenade, an open-air pedestrian street; and Centropark, an 8-hectare landscaped leisure park with restaurants and cafes, theaters and performance venues.

Anchored by three premier department stores and trading on two levels, the retail center showcases some 200 small shops and up to 15 mid-sized stores. The center has been conceived of as an animated urban passage, with the transition of major spaces on either end into landscaped garden courts. Characterized by an architecture reminiscent of botanical gardens, the courts provide not only classic shopping but also a brief respite for the shopper with cafes and tea houses.

An open-air street of restaurants and public amenities, the Promenade, recalls the great traditions of the European High Street. The Promenade is anchored to the north by a Warner Bros. multiplex cinema, also designed by RTKL, and includes Planet Hollywood and a centrally located micro-brewery.

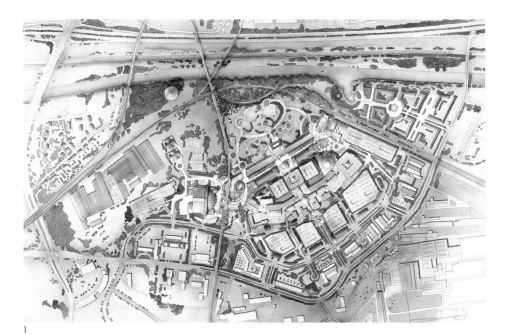

1

2

1   Site plan
2   Main entry
3   Process sketch
4   Elevation detail
5   Warner Bros. multiplex cinema
6   Construction February 1996
7   The Promenade

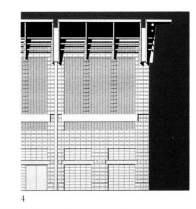

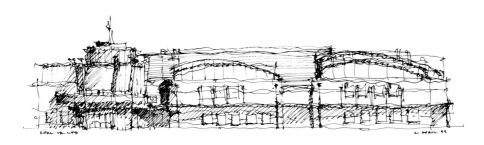

3

5

6

7

Centro Comercial Diagonal Mar

Design/Completion 1991/1998
Barcelona, Spain
Diagonal Mar, S.A.
Associate Architect: Sereland S.A.
90,000 square meters GLA
Stone and granite cladding on poured concrete structure

Overlooking the Mediterranean Sea, Diagonal Mar is the retail core of an extraordinary urban mixed-use project that also includes offices, residential, and civic buildings as well as parks and recreational facilities.

The center will have 200 specialty shops and restaurants anchored by one of Europe's most popular hypermarkets and a 24-screen cinema that will be the largest complex of its kind in Europe. A unique feature of the project is the 7,000-square-meter Terraza, an open-air civic plaza in the grand Spanish tradition of the Plaza Réal in Barcelona and the Plaza Mayor in Madrid. The Terraza will be enlivened with palm trees, fountains, and gathering spaces surrounded by a collection of popular bars and restaurants.

With fluid, wave-like glass forms played against solid, geometric shapes and volumes made of granite, marble, and limestone, RTKL's design for Diagonal Mar Centro Comercial recalls the relationship between the ever-changing aspects of the sea and the constant, stoic nature of the land.

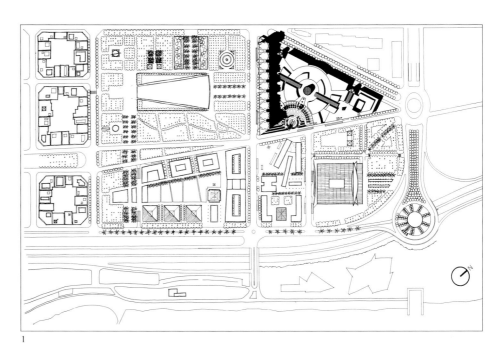

1

2

3

1 Site plan
2 The Terraza
3 Artist's perspective
4 North elevation

4

The Galleria Morley

Design/Completion 1992/1994
Perth, Australia
Coles Myer Properties Ltd and Colonial Mutual Life
Assurance Society Ltd
Associate Architect: Buchan Group of Architects
60,000 square meters

This new RTKL-designed shopping center
will include five major department/retail
stores, a multi-cinema complex, specialty
shops on two levels, a 600-seat food court,
and a 1,000-square-meter library.

The major focal point of The Galleria
Morley is the central atrium, a 30-meter-
wide octagonal courtyard in the heart of
the project. A large fountain pool at its
hub will provide a patio-style venue for
meeting friends and relaxing at umbrellaed
tables.

Potentially the leading regional retail and
entertainment center in Perth, this
shopping center provides not only high-
quality retailing but also a community
gathering place and entertainment and
leisure facilities.

1

1　Main retail corridor
2　Main entrance
3　Exterior signage
4　Central skylight

2

3

4

Lenox Square Mall

Design/Completion 1993/1995
Atlanta, Georgia
Corporate Property Investors
Steel
Brick, masonry and glazed curtain wall

Constructed as an open-air retail mall in the 1950s, Lenox Square Mall had been subjected to a variety of expansions and renovation, leaving the project visually disjointed. This, combined with the rapid growth of surrounding development, completion of the Lenox Square MARTA Station, and expansion of the competing Phipps Plaza, has necessitated comprehensive expansion and renovation.

Initial planning and urban design of the project included an analysis of the Buckhead business and residential districts with respect to area influences, land-use relationships and site dynamics such as access, density, pedestrian linkages, pedestrian and vehicular circulation.

Key to the expansion/renovation is a second-level overbuild running the length of the center, adding 170,000 square feet of GLA. The project also includes interior town squares at each anchor store entrance, connecting galleries, an expanded food court, and new exterior arcades and garage entrances.

1

1   The Obelisk
2   View of main retail corridor
3   Atrium staircase
4   Upper level

2

3

4

Roosevelt Field Mall

Design/Completion 1991/1993
Garden City, New York
Corporate Property Investors
2.5 million square feet
Composite structure
Curtain wall and stone finishes

RTKL's comprehensive expansion/renovation program has repositioned this premiere super-regional retail center. Originally designed in the 1950s, the existing single-level center comprised 2.3 million square feet of space, including four anchor department stores. Because the project's already large size and tight site constraints precluded significant growth, RTKL's plan selectively eliminated specific areas of the existing mall in order to meet the client's requirement for a planned second-level expansion.

The mall's expansion includes a new food court, additional retail space, and second-level connections to all four anchor stores. The refurbishment upgraded finishes, expanded and improved feature courts, and introduced new graphics and signage.

The new food court was designed in a unique racetrack configuration to respond to the mall's double-loaded corridor layout. It is enhanced by a system of colorful environmental graphics and directional signage, drawing shoppers into the space.

1

1   View toward Macy's
2   View of Zeppelin food court
3   Elevator
4   Staircase detail

2

3

4

Towson Town Center

Design/Completion 1984/1990
Towson, Maryland
The Hahn Company in partnership with DeChiaro Associates and Santa Anita Realty Enterprises, Inc.
939,000 square feet GLA
Steel
Pre-cast panels and masonry facade

This comprehensive expansion and renovation draw their design inspiration from 19th century European glass conservatories as well as traditional public gardens in England, Maryland, and Pennsylvania.

Anchored by Nordstrom and Hecht's department stores, the mall features 200 specialty shops, a food court, and structured parking for 4,360 cars. Two barrel-vaulted skylights, three new atrium domes, lush landscaping inside and out, and rich finishes such as terrazzo flooring, cherry and glass handrails, etched glass, and ornate columns are in keeping with the center's high-end tenants and affluent suburban Baltimore target market.

Palm trees and garden elements are used graphically and literally to reflect a garden theme throughout the mall. Weathered verdigris sculptures of mythological figures and imaginative animal hybrids lend a whimsical focus to the interior.

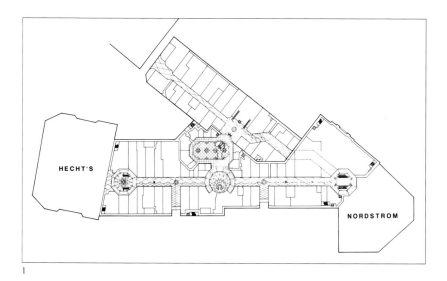

1

2

3

4

5

Tysons Corner Center

Design/Completion 1983/1986
McLean, Virginia
The Lehndorff Tysons Joint Venture
1.85 million square feet
Steel
Marble floors and brick exterior

Expanding Tysons Corner Center from below rather than above was the key to this successful complex renovation. The approach doubled the center's gross leasable area by converting an existing lower-level truck tunnel and service basement into a second level of retail.

Major excavation was required around nearly two-thirds of the building to expose the former basement level to the outside, providing the ground level entrances critical to its success as a new retail area.

In what has since become a prototype of mall refurbishment, RTKL developed a construction sequencing and phasing program that allowed the mall to remain in operation while renovation was in progress. All heavy construction occurred at non-trading hours, with elaborately decorated barricades protecting stores at night and customers during the day.

1

1   Retail mall
2   Wavy bench and landscaping
3   Main retail space

After the construction of new service areas at the perimeter of the project, new columns were placed in the service tunnel, with upper level columns added to the existing roof. Once the skylights had been added above the roof, the old roof was removed and lowered into waiting trucks and carted away. After substantial completion of the new upper level ceiling and skylight treatment, the existing mall floors were removed under barricades in the middle of the mall.

The skylight was constructed over the existing roof, allowing the mall to remain watertight during construction. The existing roof was then removed from within after mall hours.

Structured parking provides 8,500 additional parking spaces to support the expanded retail area.

2

3

The Westchester

Design/Completion 1991/1995
White Plains, New York
The O'Connor Group
1.1 million square feet
Composite structure
Architectural pre-cast and brick cladding

RTKL's design challenge was to create a new three-level retail mall, one that will serve as a "Gateway to the City," constructed atop a two-level parking garage in a tight urban site.

Anchored by an existing Neiman Marcus store and a new Nordstrom department store, The Westchester is characterized by simple details and subdued designs that enhance the shops and provide a strong upscale backdrop.

The center's interior features a two- and three-level mall space designed in a neo-classical motif, with a rich palette of materials including marble flooring, clerestory windows and skylights.

Parking facilities in this busy downtown area have been a primary planning and design consideration for the project, and the new construction includes over 3,400 spaces of structured parking. RTKL's design visually minimizes the bulk of the parking structures while also utilizing strong graphic and signage elements to direct approaching drivers to the primary parking entrances.

1

1 Main entry
2 Three-level retail space
3 Central court
4 Secondary entry
5 Stacked floor plan

2

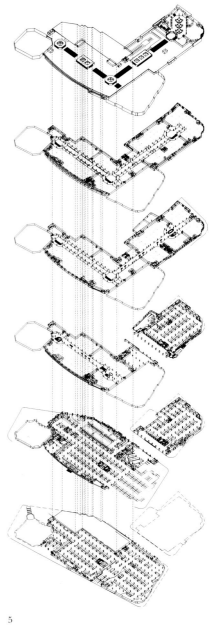

5

3

4

Valencia Town Center

Design/Completion 1990/1994
Valencia, California
Valencia Town Center Associates, L.P.
The Newhall Land & Farming Co., and JMB Retail Properties Co.
287,000 square feet

This new two-level, enclosed retail center north of Los Angeles creates a "town center" for the city of Valencia, blending into its hillside surroundings while maximizing the site's natural land forms and landscape. Architecturally, the project integrates historical references of the Santa Clarita Valley and harmoniously melds the Mission and Victorian influences indigenous to central Californian coastal communities.

Its Mediterranean exterior is a collection of towers and sloped terra cotta tile roof forms. Anchor tenants occupy spaces that resemble angular mountains. A trellised open-air rotunda with louvered roof and a central skylit gabled roof recall Victorian Fair buildings and evoke the bright festive atmosphere of England's c. 1851 Crystal Palace. A bubbling fountain and custom-designed period carousel enhance this focal point of the central plaza.

As axial terminus for Valencia's planned urban "main street," the center's Town Plaza serves as an entertainment gathering spot with restaurants, eight-screen cineplex, indoor food court, and family entertainment.

1

2

1   Central court
2   Floor clock

Eastland Shopping Centre

Design/Completion 1991/1995
Melbourne, Australia
Coles Myer Properties, Ltd
Associate Architect: Tompkins, Shaw & Evans Pty Ltd
50,500-square-meter renovation and expansion of an existing retail center, addition of a 600-seat food court, specialty stores, a fresh food hall, Coles supermarket, a Safeway and K-Mart, and a new parking structure

To allow for maximum leasing flexibility within the two-level specialty areas, RTKL developed a column-free racetrack design. A glass-domed, three-level central court and two side courts, featuring domes with painted murals, serve as gateways to the shopping areas. Quality materials and details, such as marble and terrazzo flooring, glass balustrades, and polished brass accents, reinforce the mall's upscale character.

Patterned after European markets, the fresh food hall has been designed with sensory appeal. Three-dimensional graphics of decorative items related to food preparation season the space and help define the food vendors located along the perimeter or in free-standing kiosks.

Envisioned as a community gathering place, The Town Square links Eastland Shopping Centre with exterior public spaces. Serving the main southern entrance and flooded with natural light from a two-tiered glass skylight, this space features an elevated stage for community events, a cappuccino bar, and an elliptical staircase enhanced by a water treatment.

1

1   Main retail corridor

Multi-use

Pentagon City

Design/Completion 1985/1988
Arlington, Virginia
Rose Associates, Inc. (office) and
Melvin Simon & Associates, Inc. (retail)
116-acre site
Granite cladding with masonry on steel structure (retail, office and hotel). Pre-cast concrete (parking garages).

Located outside Washington, DC, Pentagon City is one of the largest, most carefully planned mixed-use communities in the Washington metropolitan area. RTKL designed Pentagon City to blend office, hotel, and retail components with existing residential to create a convenient working/living/shopping environment within the community.

In addition to the Ritz-Carlton hotel and RTKL-designed Washington Tower office building, Pentagon City includes the 809,000-square-foot Fashion Centre at Pentagon City, also designed by RTKL and anchored by Macy's and Nordstrom.

A Metro stop within Pentagon City links the development to downtown Washington, National Airport, and existing commercial centers. Future phases of Pentagon City will include approximately 5,680 residential units. An 11-acre wooded area within the site has been turned over to Arlington County for development as a public park.

1

0   100ft   N

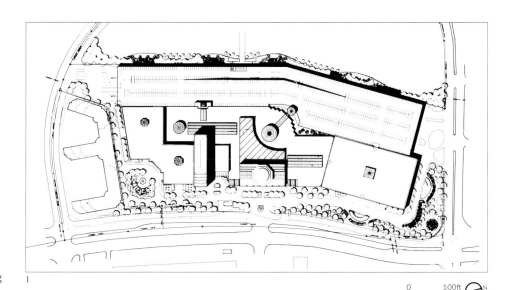

2

3

4

5

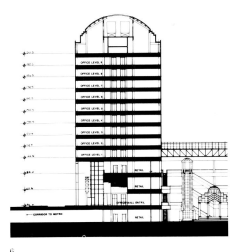

6

1   Site plan
2   Exterior view of retail, hotel, and office
3   Panorama of central atrium
4   View toward Nordstrom
5   Entry canopy detail
6   Section

Rama III

Design/Completion 1992/1998
Bangkok, Thailand
Estate Development Company Ltd and Central Department Stores
Associate Architect: Plan Architect Co. Ltd
65,000 square meters
Cast-in-place concrete structure
Brick infill with stone and metal cladding; floor material varies from
multi-colored terrazzo, ceramic tile to marble; angled structural
columns and large roughed-steel trusses

Incorporating colorful graphic images into bold and playful architectural forms, RTKL's design creates a powerful statement adjacent to one of Bangkok's major expressways.

A seven-level retail and entertainment podium comprises the first phase of the project. Later phases may include two or three 40-story residential condominiums of 600 units each, landscaped terraces, and tenant amenities.

Within the podium and connected by four distinct interior courts are a 25,000-square-meter Central Department Store, 40,000 square meters of specialty retail, supermarket, cinemas, food court, and an indoor and outdoor children's playland. A 10-story parking structure directly adjacent in addition to underground parking allows shoppers to enter the project at nearly every level.

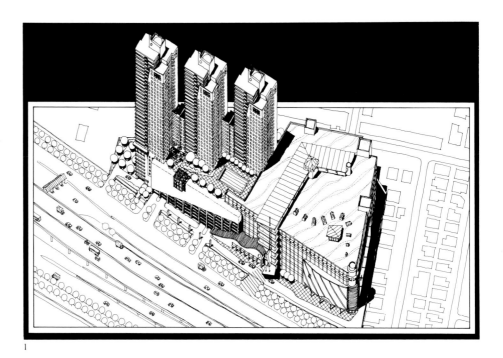

1

1   Isometric view
2   Central atrium
3   View of entry
4   Animation series of sketches
5   Southeast elevation

2

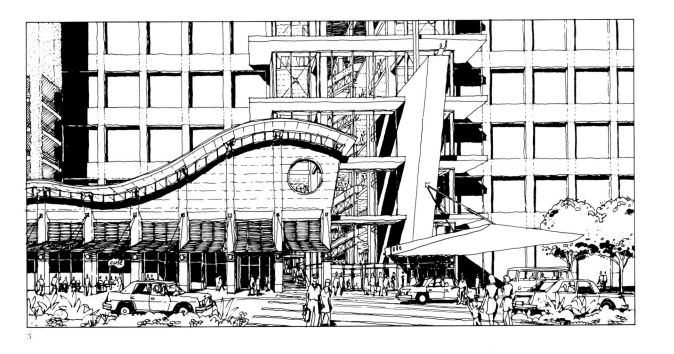

3

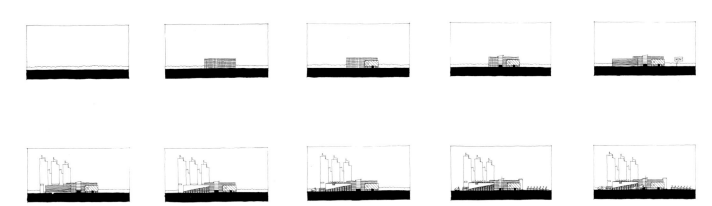

4

5

Reston Town Center

Design/Completion 1987/1990
Reston, Virginia
Reston Town Center Associates
Site area: 15 acres
Steel
Textured pre-cast panels

RTKL's competition-winning architecture for Phase One of Reston Town Center meets the community's growing demand for commercial development while evoking a contemporary "Main Street" character. The four-block Phase One encompasses two 250,000-square-foot office buildings, a 510-room Hyatt Regency hotel, 150,000 square feet of retail and cinemas, and a new open-air pavilion.

The mirror-image, 11-story office buildings form an appropriate gateway to the development and the beginnings of a recognizable skyline for Reston Town Center. The profile of the towers and the individualized facades of the street-level shops echo the picturesque quality of old Reston. The office buildings rise from two-story podiums of retail shops, their lobbies distinguished by five types of marble and natural cherry walls.

A variety of materials, an irregular massing scheme, and a full palette of texture and color give the Phase One components a common identity yet a stimulating degree of variation in appearance.

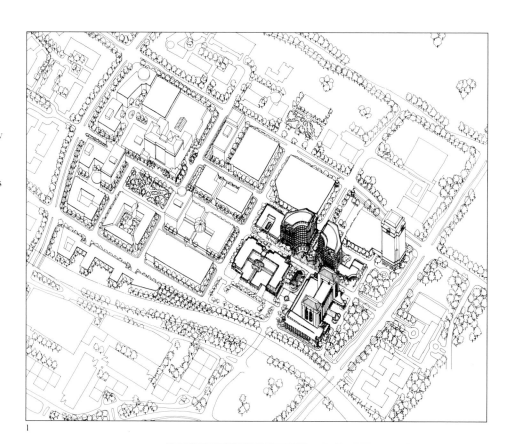

1

2

3

1 Axonometric of total development
2 Office building entry
3 Market Street
4 Environmental graphics detail
5 Fountain Square

4

5

Sun DongAn Plaza

Design/Completion 1994/1997
Beijing, China
The DongAn Group and Sun Hung Kai Properties Limited, a joint venture
Associate Architects: Institute of Project Planning & Research,
Ministry of Machinery & Electronics Industries, Wong & Tung International Ltd
Design Consultant: Architectural Design & Research Institute,
Tsing Hua University
210,000-square-foot site
Exterior facade of indigenous stone with metal accents incorporated in trellis
and canopy; traditional roof forms in tile

In the heart of the Wang Fu Jing District of Beijing, Sun DongAn Plaza is one of China's most famous retail locations. RTKL's redevelopment plan includes more than 1.5 million square feet of gross floor area, making the market the largest shopping center in Beijing and one of the largest in China.

The new Sun DongAn Plaza includes six retail levels (one below ground) containing two department stores, shops, food court, restaurants, banquet hall, cinema, and other entertainment venues. Six levels of office space will rise above the retail podium. New streetfront shops will be located at the southern end of the site.

As one of first sino-foreign joint ventures to receive a retail license in China, the venture has also received rare permission to import up to 30 percent of its merchandise. A symbol of China's open-door policy, the Sun DongAn redevelopment plan has been enthusiastically endorsed by both municipal and central government.

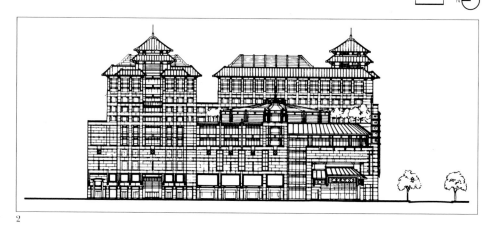

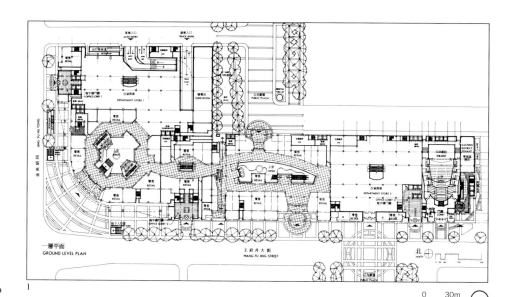

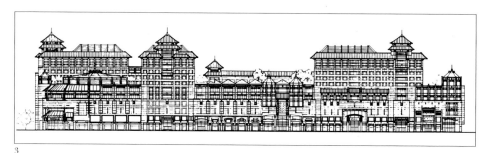

1 Ground level plan
2 North elevation
3 West elevation
4 Process sketches
5 View of model

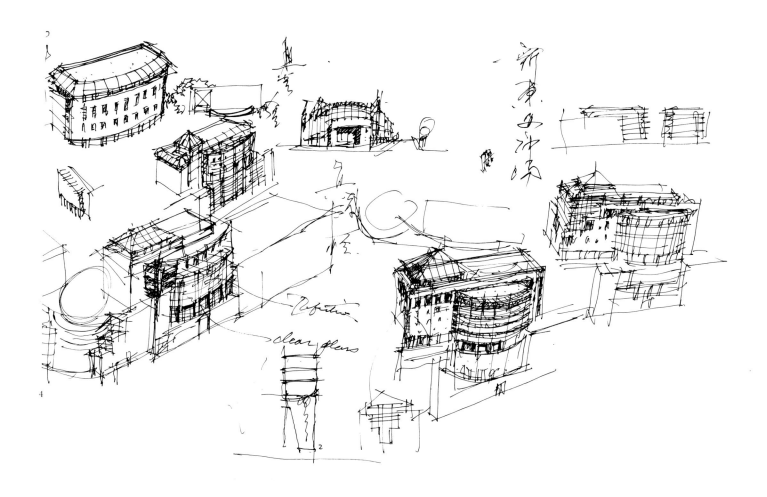

4

5

Tower City Center

Design/Completion 1983/1990
Cleveland, Ohio
Tower City Development (a subsidiary of Forest City Enterprises)
1928 historical structure
Clay tile with original tile, limestone and brick

Tower City Center is one of the most ambitious urban development efforts ever undertaken in the United States. Comprising the 350,000-square-foot Avenue retail mall, 300,000-square-foot Skylight Office Tower, and 209-room Ritz-Carlton, this waterfront mixed-use center is structured around the redevelopment of Cleveland's historic Terminal Tower.

Located within the historic train station and above an existing transit stop, The Avenue's main concourse and two new levels of retail space, multi-plex cinema, and 1,200-seat food court are enclosed by a new barrel-vaulted skylight. RTKL retained many of the station's original materials and details to evoke a traditional character that enhances the contemporary design. The new office building and hotel, built on the original 1930s foundations, complement the surrounding architecture.

RTKL's design of Tower City Center maximizes connections among all three components to create a synergy and establish important links to the city's rejuvenated central business district.

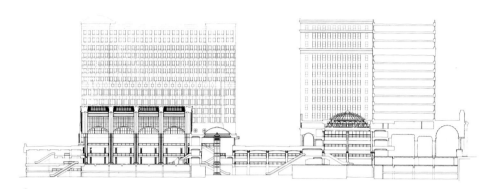

1

2

3

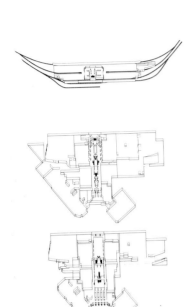

4

5

6

7

8

Urbano Alameda

Design/Completion 1985/1998
Mexico City, Mexico
Grupo Arlette
Associate Architect: Grupo Dahnos
275,000 square feet
Steel
Glazed curtain wall and stone finishes

Strategically placed between the financial district and the historic Zocalo (town plaza), Urbano Alameda is an important part of the revitalization of an area heavily damaged in the 1985 earthquake. This mixed-use project represents the first phase of the 13-block Alameda Plaza redevelopment plan.

The complex includes retail space in the three-level building base, a 15-level office tower, 1,050 structured parking spaces (four above- and four below-grade decks), and a restaurant with an outdoor dining terrace on the upper two levels. The retail base opens onto a large, stone-paved public plaza which meets the Avenida Juárez with a canopy of trees. Dramatic night-time lighting plays a significant role in attracting pedestrian activity.

Architecturally the project is distinctive yet responsive to the surrounding area which includes the Alameda Park and the adjacent circa 1930s British Petroleum headquarters. Simple forms and massing anchor the project to its context, while natural stone, tile, and metals are used throughout to reflect the locale.

1

1   Elevation/plan

City Plaza

Design 1995
Taegu, Korea
Confidential
100,000-square-meter site with a future subway line
and 5,000 parking spaces

RTKL's master plan for City Plaza creatively redevelops an existing textile factory site into a vibrant, social and commercial hub. Based on extensive market research and demographic studies, the plan has been conceived to respond specifically to the future needs of the city of Taegu, Korea.

The plan is organised around a series of compact urban districts, each providing a distinct facility or service for the city: retail, catering and fashion; entertainment; museums and cultural arts; electronics and communications; sports and health; offices and hotels.

At the heart of this urban project is the City Plaza Dome, a dramatic central public space. Over 100 meters in diameter, the glass dome covers a terraced plaza, creating one of the most spectacular outdoor spaces in Korea. Dramatically engaging visitors, a giant video wall in the entry plaza will project unparalleled coverage of activities within the plaza, the country, or anywhere in the world. Encircling this area are the various districts, expressed in disparate architectural vocabulary and each linked via arcaded streets.

1

1   View of model

Washington Center

Design/Completion 1986/1989
Washington, DC
Quadrangle Development Corporation
400,000 square feet (office building), 900-room hotel;
historic refurbishment; 500 parking spaces
Steel and concrete
Stone and pre-cast panel facades; refurbished terra cotta building

Located south of the Washington Convention Center, this urban multi-use development covers a full city block and includes an office building (which incorporates the restoration of the c. 1911 McLachlen Bank building), the Grand Hyatt Washington hotel, street-level retail, and parking on five below-grade levels.

Linked directly to the Metro Center subway stop, the office building features a 12-story skylit atrium enclosed by landscaped balconies on three sides and a dramatic window-wall building entrance on 11th Street.

To integrate the building into the surrounding community, RTKL employed a design vocabulary consistent with that of the historic McLachlen building.

The Washington Center–Grand Hyatt Washington site played a pivotal role in the rejuvenation of Washington's "old" downtown. The complex helped meet growing office space requirements in the area, serves as the convention center's "official hotel," and provides links between the convention center and the Metro system.

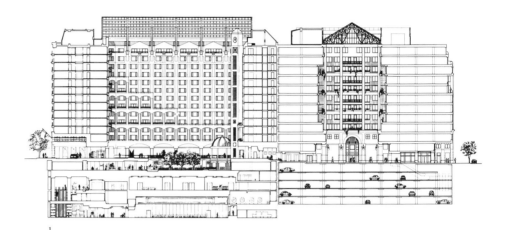

1

2

1 Section
2 Office lobby
3 Elevator vestibule
4 Cornice line of McLachlen building
5 Office entry

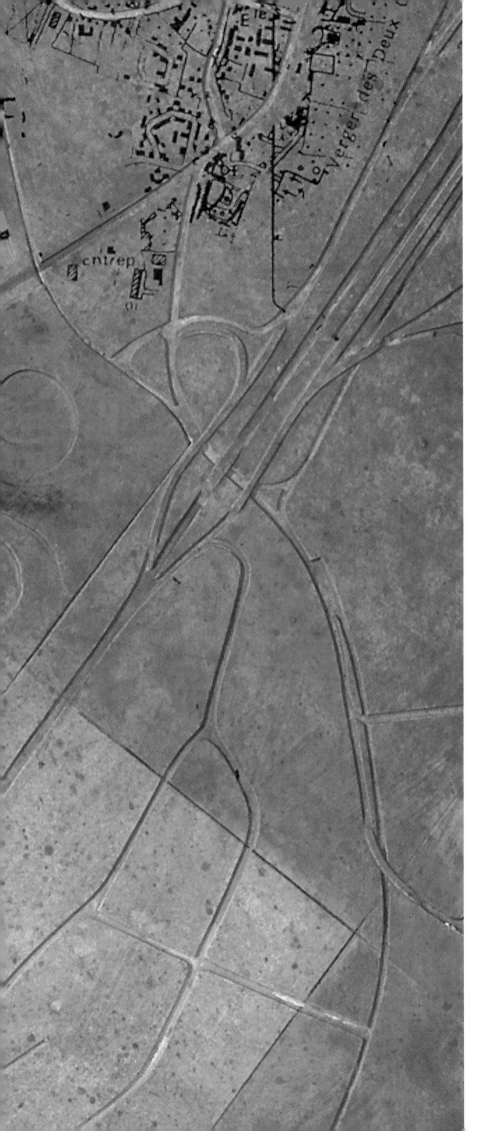

Planning/
Urban Design

Cincinnati 2000

Design/Completion 1978/1979
Cincinnati, Ohio
City of Cincinnati
Urban regeneration plan for a 30-block area

Cincinnati 2000, RTKL's update plan for the development of downtown Cincinnati, builds upon the firm's 1960s master plans for the downtown and the riverfront. Implemented over a period of 20 years, the plans for the area began the process of reuniting the city with its riverfront and created such world-renowned public spaces as Fountain Square.

Heading a multi-disciplinary team of planning, transportation, and economic consultants, RTKL created a comprehensive and flexible plan that allows for expansion and intensification of diversified urban activities through the end of the century. To stimulate both day and night-time use, the plan provides for increased residential development within the core, as well as offices, retail, hotels, business services, and cultural activities.

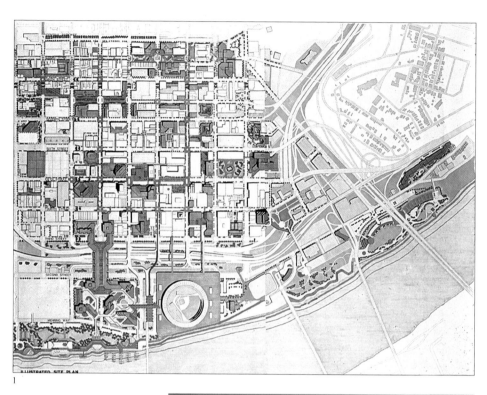
1

1   Urban master plan
2   Fountain Square

2

Montgomery Village

Design 1970
Montgomery County, Maryland
Kettler Brothers, Inc.
2,300-acre new town master plan

Home to nearly 30,000 people, Montgomery Village is still considered one of the most successful new town developments during the explosion of growth in the US suburbs of the 1960s and 1970s.

A county ordinance establishing a residential density of 15 persons per gross acre allowed RTKL and Kettler Brothers to dedicate school sites, build major roads, bury utility lines, and set aside over 25 per cent of the land as open space. Natural beauty was preserved, recreation opportunities created, and business, service, and shopping areas set aside.

One of Montgomery Village's strengths is its ability to respond to change. RTKL's flexible plan has undergone modifications as changing consumer preferences have led developers to modify planned high-rise residential communities and shift to more moderate-density housing within lower structures.

Montgomery Village's continuing success is demonstrated by its long-term growth, timeless appearance, range of home styles and prices, and community stability.

1 Garden apartments
2 Master Plan
3 Aerial view

1

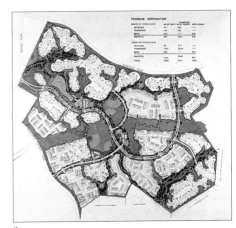

2

3

Camden Yards Sports Complex

Design/Completion 1989/1992
Baltimore, Maryland
Maryland Stadium Authority and HOK Sports Facilities Group
85-acre urban site

RTKL's masterplan and urban design for this site near Baltimore's Inner Harbor set the stage for the new 47,000-seat Oriole Park at Camden Yards, a state-of-the-art baseball stadium with the character of a traditional urban ballpark. As masterplanning coordinator and urban design consultant, RTKL created a comprehensive development plan and guidelines for both the ballpark, designed by HOK Sports Facilities Group, and a future football stadium.

Planned to make strong visual and physical connections to the city fabric, the site integrates light rail and incorporates new public spaces that serve as gateways to the city. The plan also addresses locations for future development as well as access, parking, and circulation issues.

RTKL's urban design input influenced the design of the complex. Examples included preserving Eutaw Street, renovating the historic train terminal, and adaptively reusing the 1,100-foot-long B&O warehouse for office and retail space and as a dramatic backdrop to the outfield.

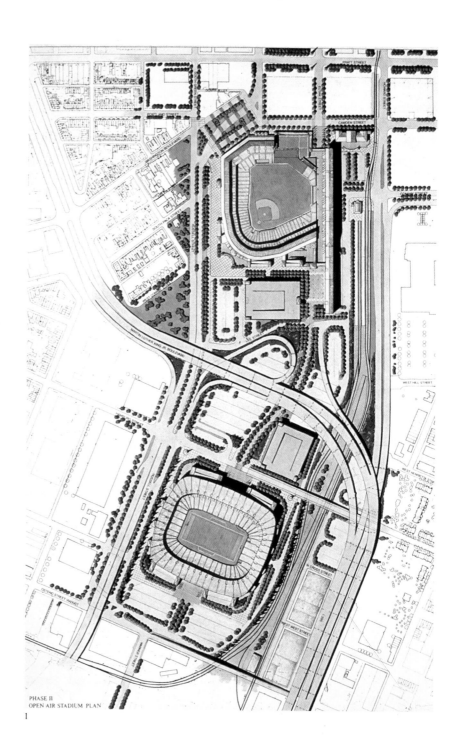

PHASE II
OPEN AIR STADIUM PLAN

1

1   Illustrative master plan
2   Figure/ground
3   Renovated B&O warehouse
4   Aerial view of the ballpark

2

3

4

Dalian New City Center

Design 1994
Liaoning Province, China
Dalian Economic and Technical Development Zone
9 square kilometers

RTKL's plan for this new town development district adjacent to Xiao Yao Bay consists of eight districts within an urban hierarchy. The central business district includes office buildings and twin 25-story signature towers fronting a main square. An entertainment district, encircled by canals, waterfront plazas, and low-rise buildings, creates a pedestrian-friendly environment. The commercial district borders on the train station, main passenger terminal, and ferry terminal center, providing a focal point for the area's commercial activities.

The focus of the recreational district is a theme park which unites Chinese culture and western technology. The hydrophilicity of Xiaoyaowan's natural landscape governs the planning principle for the residential district with high-, medium- and low-density housing offering water links and views to the sea.

In addition to the sports center, which encompasses an indoor sporting arena, the remaining districts incorporate a world trade tower, aquarium, oceanic museum, conference center, art gallery, outdoor theater, and several city parks.

1

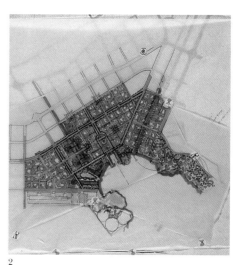

2

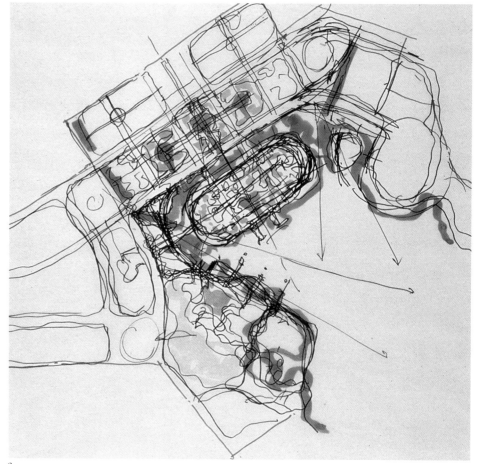

3

1   Process sketch A
2   Process sketch B
3   Process sketch C
4&5   Model view

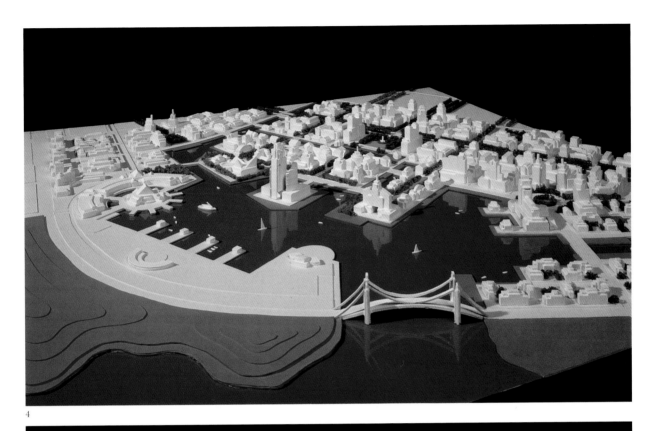

4

5

Huangshan Furong International Tourist Town

Design 1993
Anhui Province, China
Huangshan Development Company, Anhui
8 square kilometers

RTKL's master plan for this proposed international tourist village creates a unique sense of place and establishes a flexible and feasible development strategy that can be implemented over the next 15 years.

The town is planned for a site on the north side of Huangshan (The Yellow Mountain), a national treasure known for its mist-shrouded peaks and natural beauty. RTKL's master plan creates five zones with distinct characters and densities (The Town, Resort zone, Conference/Technical Village, Cultural Village and Residential Village).

The town center is located on an island in a river running through the site. The resort zone will include a golf course, fitness facilities, honeymoon village, and hillside and lakeside hotels. The conference/technical center will attract international exhibitions, while the cultural village will feature the local folk art, Chinese painting and calligraphy, and tea houses and gardens. The residential district will encompass a variety of housing types.

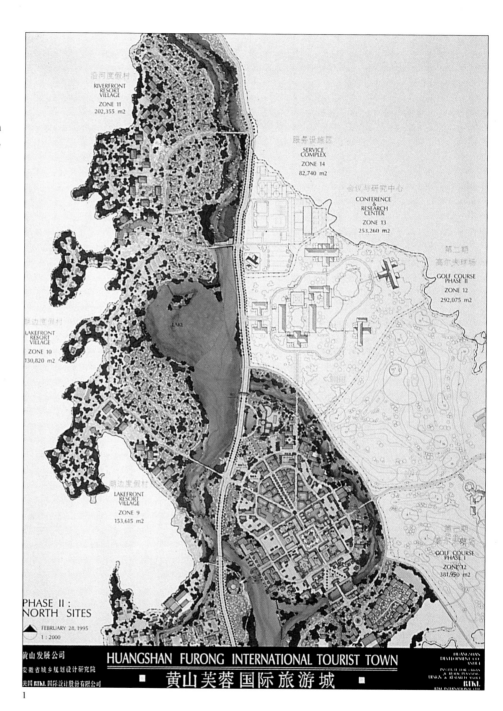

1   Site master plan
2   Marketplace
3   Village Square

2

3

Shae-Zee Island

Design/Completion 1992/1993
Shae-Zee Island, Taipei, Taiwan
Taipei Department of City Planning
Associate Planner: Kaichuan Engineering Consultant Co., Ltd
320 hectares

Selected by invited competition, RTKL and an international team of consultants provided design services for the redevelopment of Shae-Zee Island, an agricultural peninsula and the largest parcel of underdeveloped land in Taipei.

The island's redevelopment is part of the largest building boom in Taipei's history and will help meet the demand for recreational and entertainment facilities generated by Taipei's growing population.

Developed through a public/private process, the plan provides a mix of entertainment, recreational, cultural, and residential uses for the island's residents and the greater metropolitan area.

Among the city's objectives are protecting ecological systems and implementing a flood-prevention plan, creating a distinct urban form to accentuate the waterfront amenities and accommodate recreation and entertainment activities, and formulating a destination that will attract domestic and international visitors.

1

2

1   Illustrative master plan
2   Harbor-side cultural district

State-Thomas Area Plan

Design 1986
Dallas, Texas
Friends of State-Thomas
100 acres

The State-Thomas Area Plan was commissioned by a coalition of property owners to guide the rezoning of a planned development district adjacent to the Dallas Central Business District.

Responding to the concerns of residents and property owners and to City Planning Department proposals, RTKL established a framework for development which greatly extended the range of housing types available in downtown Dallas.

The study area encompasses a city-designed historic district of Victorian houses as well as substantially vacant land with a mixture of retail, office and medium-density residential zoning.

Plan development involved frequent meetings over a one-year period with neighborhood residents, property owners, City staff members and concerned community organizations. The planned development ordinance was approved by the City Council in March 1986.

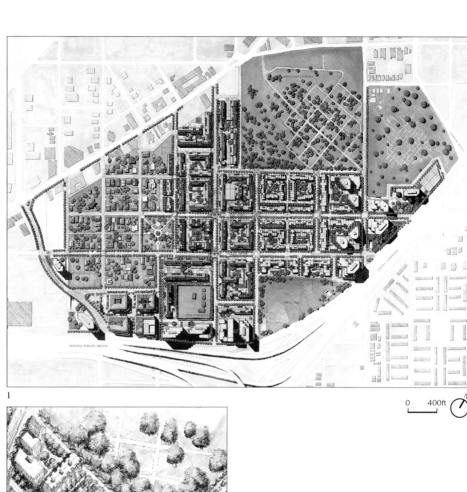

1

0   400ft

2

1   Area plan
2   Isometric view

Stadtquartier Lehrter Bahnhof

Design 1994
Berlin, Germany
Tishman Speyer Properties of Berlin LP
Associate Architect: Architekten Sattler
15 hectares

RTKL's urban design proposal in this limited competition brings unity to a variety of sub-districts of mid-city Berlin—the new government buildings designed by Axel Shultes to the south, a recognized business district, existing residential to the north, the Humboldthafen waterfront to the east, and the Alt-Moabit to the southwest.

The plan's overall macro order embraces the fabric of Shultes' Band des Bundes south of the Spreebogen. While the linear complex of buildings creates the essence of an orthogonal grid, defining formal spaces and ceremonial boulevards, RTKL have extrapolated the grid northward. This integrates the government buildings into the stadtquartier, links it with the new Lehrter Bahnhof, and unifies a mixture of uses and districts throughout the site.

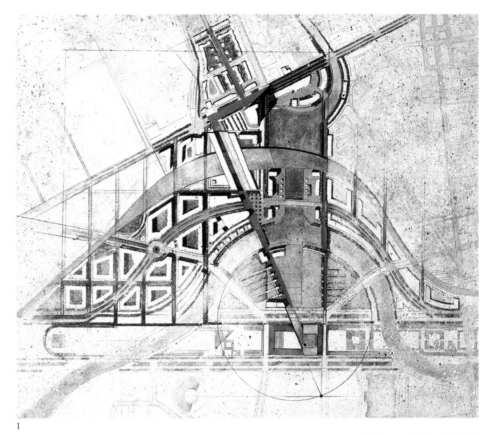

1

2

The arcing geometry of the Spreebogen, echoed by the curve of the S-Bahn viaduct, bisects the grid; but these organic shapes are seen not as a contradiction to the order established by Shultes but as an integral element to the overall urban fabric. This interplay creates a type of urbanistic tension which lends the plan cohesion. The plan reinforces the unifying aspects of these major elements by introducing a third central arc through the site—a formal curving boulevard which mirrors the bend of the Spree.

3

5

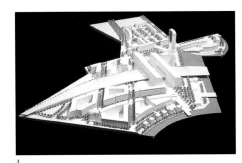

4

Old San Juan Waterfront

Design/Completion 1990/1998
San Juan, Puerto Rico
Paseo Portuario SE, a joint venture of Rexach Construction Company
and Plaza Las Americas
Associate Architect: Milton M. Ruiz & Associates
Seven block district to include retail, office, hotel, casino,
and residential uses

RTKL provided urban design and
architectural services as a member of the
design and development team selected to
create a new commercial and residential
core adjacent to the cruise ship terminals
of Old San Juan.

The development focuses on Calle La
Marina, the major pedestrian boulevard
along the bay, and the creation of Paseo
Colon, a new street perpendicular to Calle
Marina extending north from the waterfront
into Old San Juan. By reinforcing the
urban street wall along Calle La Marina
with a new precinct of buildings, the
project creates a cohesive urban edge.
A traditional entry sequence from the
waterfront into the city is reintroduced by
the new Paseo Colon.

The intersection of Calle La Marina and
Paseo Colon is celebrated by a new
"polyartistic" observation tower that will
combine music, lighting, and interactive
artistic events. At the tower's base, an
electronic map of Old San Juan will be
installed in the street paving.

The project received a 1991 Citation for
Excellence in Urban Design from the
American Institute of Architects.

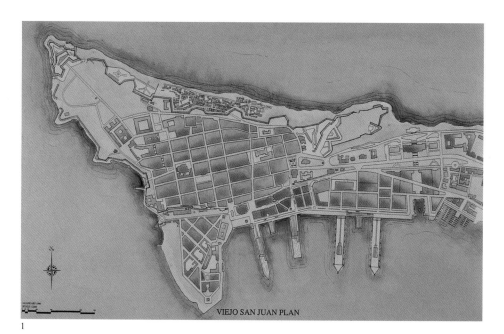

VIEJO SAN JUAN PLAN

1

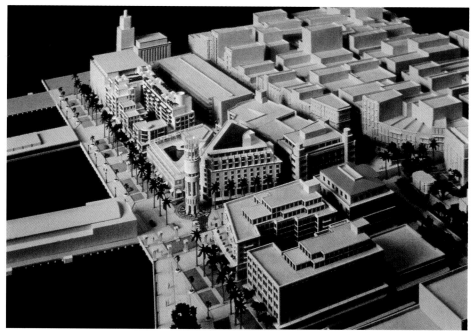

2

1   Area figure/ground
2   Model view
3   Calle La Marina

3

Euro Val d'Oise

Design 1992
Roissy, France
Euro Val d'Oise Association
Site area: 2,500 acres

RTKL was one of five international teams invited to participate in an "ideas competition" for this strategic site near Paris' Charles de Gaulle Airport. The currently undeveloped area is identified as an "international activities park" in the master plan for the Paris region.

Competing teams attempted to create an identity for this important sector of Paris, while also structuring an urban development that achieved a balance between housing, employment, and the environment.

1

2

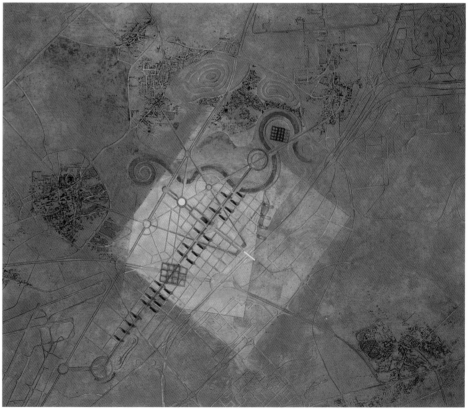

3

1   Site plan
2   Site model
3   Area plan

Harbor Town, Mud Island

Design/Completion 1988/1990
Memphis, Tennessee
Island Property Associates
110-acre site with 800 residential units

RTKL masterplanned Harbor Town as a traditional community—a low-rise residential village that includes a range of dwelling units supported by service retail, a small inn, marina, and yacht club.

The village is organized by a traditional street grid, offset by a series of diagonal boulevards which define the various single-family, multi-family, and commercial neighborhoods. The plan reflects a scaled-down urban fabric derivative of Memphis, with houses located close to tree-lined streets, small common greens, and boulevards with medians.

Architecturally, Harbor Town's residential and retail buildings contain elements such as low-pitched roofs, front porches, balconies, and elevated entries, indigenous to the Memphis region and evocative of early harbor towns. Special attention to architectural style, building type, and streetscape and landscape design enhances the island's character and contributes to the image of community.

1

2

3

1   Illustrative master plan
2&3   Public park

Interior Architecture

AT&T Customer Technology Center

Design/Completion 1987/1988
The Infomart, Dallas, Texas
AT&T Real Estate
35,000 square feet
Pre-cast columns
Natural materials, glass and stainless steel

Designed to showcase for AT&T's products and services, the project consists of four distinct functional areas: the showroom, an executive briefing center, a client education and training center, and administrative offices.

The designers focused on creating a technically advanced, functional space that does not intimidate the consumer or overwhelm the product. The space is also flexible enough to respond to future product displays.

Used in innovative fashions, standard, durable materials were selected for their ability to bear up under a high volume of traffic. The floors are made of industrial end block wood; perforated steel and handrubbed plaster are used for wall finishes. Stainless steel, aluminum, and cherry wood finishes are used throughout.

1

1 Main reception area
2 Reception area

2

92

Bank One Cleveland Offices

Design/Completion 1990/1991
Cleveland, Ohio
Bank One Corporation
185,000 square feet

The regional headquarters offices for Bank One, Cleveland are housed in the RTKL-designed Bank One Center, located in the heart of downtown Cleveland's financial district. Programmed, planned, and designed by RTKL, the facilities include a branch banking lobby, executive offices for the Trust and Administration groups, and 85,000 square feet of non-customer-contact departmental facilities, all located on six floors of the office tower.

In designing the new space, RTKL created a progressive consumer-oriented image for the bank lobby and executive areas. Reflecting the functional needs of the non-customer-contact functions, each floor was designed with a reception and conference center at the point of customer contact and a functional core for service and filing needs. Open office systems were utilized throughout to provide optimum flexibility.

1

2

1 Main lobby
2 Main entry

Dykema Gossett

Design/Completion 1993/1993
Washington, DC
Dykema Gossett
15,000 square feet
Materials include Minnesota limestone, Australian lacewood, Sapeli
mahogany, Italian marble, etched glass, and brushed bronze

Conveying a traditional atmosphere without resorting to literal classical stereotypes was the design challenge for the Washington offices of Dykema Gossett, Michigan's largest law firm.

In creating a transitional design that reflects the firm's Midwestern origins, RTKL applied the state university's blue and gold colors, adding olive green for distinction. Strong horizontal and vertical planes give geometric definition to the full-floor offices. Traditional forms such as pilasters and wainscoting are interpreted in a fresh, contemporary idiom with wood, metal, stone, and glass.

Inspired by the window wall of the base building, four-inch-wide wainscoting serves as a consistent point of reference throughout the office space. The motif is executed in wood in the elevator lobby and reception areas, in fabric-wrapped panels in the conference rooms, and again with wood in the predominantly glass wall of the library. In the reception area, a wood screen with sandblasted glass provides visual and auditory privacy for both receptionist and visitors.

1

2

1   Reception seating
2   Reception

Legg Mason Wood Walker, Inc.

Design/Completion 1992/1993
Legg Mason Wood Walker, Inc.
Philadelphia, Pennsylvania
65,000 square feet

Located in Center City Philadelphia, the new Legg Mason offices reflect the application of RTKL's modular prototype, developed for two dozen regional offices.

The prototype is being used to achieve a consistent corporate style as branch offices move to new quarters or renovate existing space. Covering layout, finishes, furniture, graphics, and equipment as well as requirements for power, communications, and personnel, the prototype design is adaptable to offices ranging from drive-in facilities to historic buildings to high-rise office space.

In Philadelphia, the application of the company-wide design standards was particularly important since the office represents the merger of two branch offices and a local development firm.

Four coordinating color palettes of materials, finishes, and furniture allow up to 16 combinations within an overall framework. A glass standard responds to Legg Mason's emphasis on visual communication between offices while standards for lighting and base and crown moldings are compatible with a variety of building types.

1

2

1   Reception area
2   Interior corridor

Embassy of Sweden

Design/Completion 1992/1994
Washington, DC
The Government of Sweden
Associate Architect: Stintzing Arkitekter, AB
30,000 square feet

RTKL provided full interior architecture and design services for the Embassy of Sweden's Washington offices.

Located on two floors, the new space houses embassy personnel and support staff and includes a multi-purpose room, library, secure storage rooms, luncheon room, and conference and reception areas.

Incorporating both Swedish and American materials, the embassy reflects Swedish aesthetic and cultural influences. It also responds to specific Swedish requirements, such as the provision of windows for every employee.

RTKL worked in conjunction with a Swedish design architect for planning and design. Also part of the team were local embassy personnel and National Property Board of Sweden representatives.

1

2

1   Main reception
2   Dining room

W.R. Grace & Co.

Design/Completion 1990/1991
Boca Raton, Florida
W.R. Grace & Co. (interior design) and
Crocker & Company (architecture)
210,000 square feet

W.R. Grace & Co., an international chemical and health-care company, relocated its New York City headquarters to an RTKL-designed office building in Boca Raton. The relocation was designed to reduce the operating costs of the headquarters facility and improve the quality of life for employees.

Moving from fewer private to more open offices, the design of the new work stations offers an efficient use of space that gives nearly the entire organization access to natural light and outdoor views.

Extensive custom-designed architectural woodwork, audio-visual, and lighting systems were used. Major special areas include a teleconferencing center, private dining facilities, rotunda and gallery spaces, a visitor center, computer rooms, and 1,000-square-foot monumental stair and reception area at executive floors.

1

2

1   Feature stair
2   Exhibition area

Coopers & Lybrand

Design/Completion 1994/1995
Tysons Corner, Virginia
Coopers & Lybrand
Interior installation of new 75,000 square-foot corporate offices

This commission for the relocation of Coopers & Lybrand's business assurance department and a portion of their government consulting and tax groups began with extensive pre-design analyses as well as an overall needs assessment. This included extensive blocking and stacking scenarios as well as projections for growth over a two- to four-year period.

The design integrates emerging trends in new business space, including a computerized hoteling system whereby staff utilize computer-touch screens at kiosks to reserve temporary office space. The kiosks forward computer, voice mail, and phone connections to the reserved office space. The offices are equipped with docking ports for notebook computers and flexible storage for files and materials that are constantly moved from office to hoteling storage.

1

2

1   Main reception
2   Main conference room

Peabody & Brown

Design/Completion 1993/1994
Washington, DC
Peabody & Brown
Interior installation of new 26,000 square-foot corporate offices
Blue lacquer accent walls, Swiss pearwood and Thai silk upholstered panels; white marble flooring and counter tops. Mahogany accents on doors and furniture.

RTKL worked closely with headquarters and local personnel in the selection and design of this Boston-based law firm's new Washington offices. After conducting two building test-fits, RTKL helped the client determine that moving, rather than renovating its existing space, would be the best solution to accommodate its growth to a 60-person office.

The new space contains private and open offices, a reception area, conference rooms, library, central filing area, employee lunchroom, and service center.

RTKL's contemporary and sophisticated interior design is in keeping with office standards already in place in the Boston headquarters and Providence, Rhode Island, office.

1

2

1   Main reception
2   Reception desk detail

The Center Club

Design/Completion 1988/1989
Baltimore, Maryland
The Center Club
23,000 square feet

RTKL's design for the relocation of The Center Club of Baltimore places it in the heart of the city's central business district, occupying one-and-a-half floors of one of Baltimore's prestigious office towers, the United States Fidelity & Guaranty Company's Light Street building.

The 23,000-square-foot facility encompasses a 210-seat dining room, cocktail lounge, grill room, and private dining and meeting rooms. RTKL provided architecture, interior architecture, mechanical and electrical engineering, graphic design, and art consultation services.

1

1   Entry to main dining room
2   Private dining room
3   The grill room
4&5   Central staircase

2

3

4

5

Hotels and Resorts

Hotel Amstel

Design Completion 1989/1992
Amsterdam, The Netherlands
InterContinental Hotels
Associate Architect: Erik Lopes Cardozo
79-room refurbishment of historic structure
Brick, timber and stone facade

RTKL's renovation of this c. 1866 hotel along the Amstel River in Amsterdam converted it from its original 111 guest rooms to a "grand luxury" 79-room, five-star hotel.

An existing addition was demolished and replaced with a new two-level brick and pre-cast stone addition which houses a 97-seat restaurant (compared with 40 prior to renovation) and leisure center with swimming pool and health club/spa.

The renovation of the seven-level hotel also includes restoration of the exterior brick, timber, and stone facade.

The Amstel was reopened in September 1992 and has since been featured in numerous publications, including *Hotels, Contract Design, Conde Nast Traveller,* and *Travel & Leisure.*

1

2

1 Night view from canal
2 Conservatory addition
3 The Grand Hall
4 Main entry
5 New pool and health club

3

4

5

Club Industrial de Monterrey

Design/Completion 1992/1995
Monterrey, Mexico
Club Industrial de Monterrey
Associate Architect: Arq. Jose Garza Gallardo and Maiz Proyectos
60,000 square feet, 5 stories
Steel
Stone and copper cladding

Nestled into its mountaintop site, with dramatic views of the region, this exclusive dining club provides a wide variety of meeting and catering options for both public and private functions.

RTKL's design organizes 60,000 square feet on five levels, with private dining rooms on the upper levels, formal dining at entry, an events hall on the lower level, and administrative functions on the mezzanine level, all to be constructed atop a plinth base housing a 350-space parking garage.

Specific design features include:

a wine cellar housed in a 45-foot-high, cone-shaped element derived from historic Mexican grain silos;

passive solar design, including louvers and screens on south and east facades, with minimal fenestration on the west facade; and building systems designed to accommodate future expansion without major disruption to the existing facility.

1

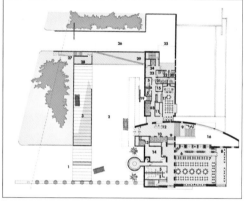

2

1   Model view
2   Ground floor plan

Tanjung Aru Resort

Design/Completion 1994/1998
Kota Kinabalu, Sabah, East Malaysia
Golden Plus Holding Berhad
500 rooms

RTKL provided masterplanning services for an oceanfront resort overlooking the South China Sea.

Sited to maximize views of the water, the components are arranged to create a courtyard that steps down to the ocean. The resort's wood frame construction mirrors the region's indigenous architecture and is enhanced through carefully planned landscaping that blurs the boundaries between interior and exterior.

Outdoor spaces are defined by heavily planted palms, flower beds, and other lush plantings.

1

2

1   Courtyard perspective
2   Site plan

Grand Hyatt Washington

Design/Completion 1986/1987
Washington, DC
Quadrangle Development Corporation
760,000 square feet, 907 rooms
Steel and concrete
Stone and pre-cast panel facades

The 13-story Grand Hyatt Washington represents the first phase of the RTKL-designed Washington Center mixed-use development across from the Washington convention center.

The hotel is distinguished by its lofty atrium courtyard, featuring unusual and extensive water features, abundant landscaping, and theatrical lighting. The hotel also includes a 18,000-square-foot main ballroom, 9,000-square-foot junior ballroom, and extensive banquet and meeting facilities. To comply with the height restrictions in Washington, the design creatively locates these back-of-house functions in five levels below grade.

Each of the hotel's luxury guest rooms offers a view of either the capital city or of the dramatically active courtyard.

1

1 Main atrium
2 Main atrium from above
3 Porte Cochere
4 View from H Street, northwest

4

2

3

Hyatt Regency Grand Cayman

Design/Completion 1985/1985
Grand Cayman Island, British West Indies
Ellesmere (Cayman) Ltd
Stucco on block facade with concrete structure

RTKL's design for the Hyatt Regency Grand Cayman hotel lends elegance to the Caribbean guest experience. The 234-room hotel is part of the Britannia Resort Complex which also includes 400 condominiums, a clubhouse, and a Jack Nicklaus-designed 18-hole golf course. The hotel's luxury rooms are arranged in a village of clustered buildings which reflects the colonial tradition of Caribbean architecture and encloses a lush tropical garden.

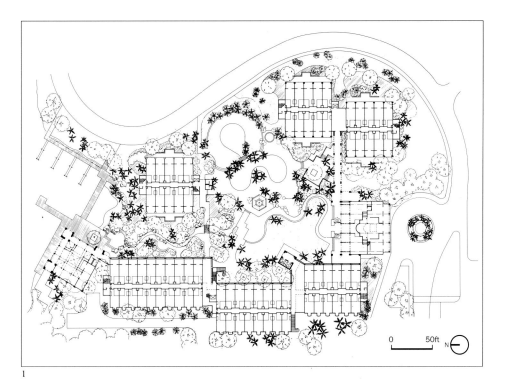

1

2

110

1   Site plan
2   The pool and deck area
3   Hotel restaurant and lobby
4   View from the golf course
5   Informal dining area

3

4

5

Harborside Hyatt Conference Center and Hotel

Design/Completion 1991/1993
Boston, Massachusetts
Logan Harborside Associates II Limited Partnership
200,000 square feet, 270 rooms
Concrete
Brick-clad facade and glazed curtain wall

Located on Bird Island Flats near the entrance to Boston Harbor, the Harborside Hyatt respects the site's waterfront location and provides excellent views of the Boston skyline and harbor islands. RTKL's design carefully "fits" the 14-story hotel into the public Harborwalk, the ferry and its dock, and the proposed Harborpoint Park.

The hotel's lighthouse form acknowledges its waterfront location at the edge of Logan Airport. In addition to the 270 guestrooms, the conference center and hotel contain a two-level open lobby, meeting rooms, a ballroom, restaurant, health club with pool, and small auditorium.

Created in the early 1970s by filling portions of Boston Harbor, Bird Island Flats has been divided into an air cargo area and three commercial development areas. The hotel and conference center zone is planned to include additional office and manufacturing buildings and parking. The other two zones are dedicated to office, research, and assembly space.

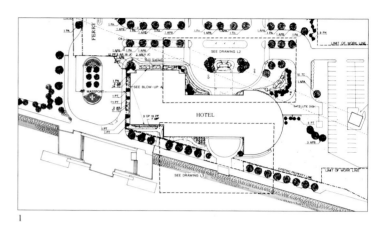

1

2

1   Site plan
2   View from the east
3   Main lobby
4   Reception and check-in

3

4

The Manhattan

Design/Completion 1988/1991
Makuhari, Chiba Prefecture, Japan
Kajima Corporation; NESCO Co Ltd
205,000 square feet (131 rooms)
Associate Architect: Kajima Corporation
Steel
Green tinted glass, white ceramic tile,
accented by polished stainless steel

RTKL's first completed building in Japan,
The Manhattan, evokes the energy and
sophistication of New York, a city that holds
special fascination for the hotel's owners.

The circular geometry of the hotel tower
responds to the street's change in
direction and serves as a landmark gateway
to the city, while a more formal and linear
eastern elevation defines the edge between
the city and the adjacent park.

The hotel's interior is characterized by
small, intimate public spaces linked by a
promenade running the entire width of
the building. Every room has a view—from
the hotel rooms and assortment of smaller
meeting rooms to the tea lounge, Japanese
restaurant, and specialty restaurant. The
southwest corner entrance offers sweeping
vistas of a picturesque boulevard on one
side and a park on the other.

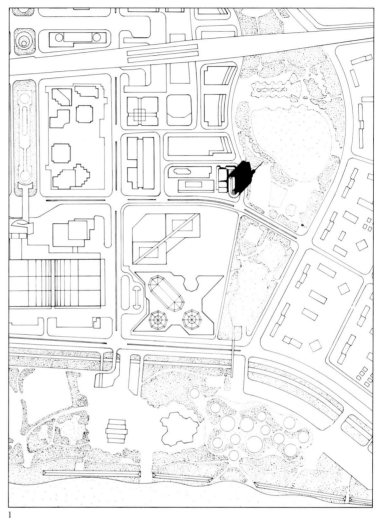

1

2

1 Site plan
2 View from the south
3 Main entry
4 View from the east
5–6 Architect's perspective
7 Ground floor plan

3

4

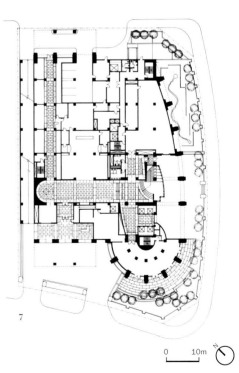

7

5

6

0   10m

St Andrews Old Course Hotel

Design/Completion 1987/1989
St Andrews, Scotland
Old Course Ltd and The Zimmer Group
Original structure
Concrete and stone cladding, slate roofs

Charged with transforming a somewhat severe existing structure into a setting befitting the birthplace of golf, RTKL led the design team for the renovation and expansion of the Old Course Hotel. Located next to the "Road Hole" of the fabled St Andrews Old Course, the hotel now boasts a dramatically improved exterior, realignment and reorganization of its interior, and an orientation that takes advantage of views to the course, the North Sea, and historic St Andrews.

The exterior renovation added a handsome, pitched slate roof and replaced existing balconies with traditional wrought-iron ones. French doors were added as well as new glazing that incorporates traditional Scottish detailing. Cast stone cornices were added for accents, and the stark concrete walls redone in harl.

On the interior, ground-floor corridors were relocated to the golf course side of the hotel to maximize views. Guest rooms on three levels were consolidated and a new ballroom/meeting room was added. A newly remodeled spa and lap pool serve as centerpiece of the resort.

1

1   View from the Bridge Hole
2   The library
3   Foyer
4   New pool and health club

116

2

3

4

The Bellevue

Design/Completion 1987/1989
Philadelphia, Pennsylvania
Richard I. Rubin & Co., Inc.
Historic renovation and conversion of existing hotel into
950,000-square foot multi-use development

RTKL transformed Philadelphia's landmark Bellevue Hotel into a mixed-use project that combines a more intimate luxury version of the hotel with upscale offices and shops.

For convenience, practicality, and privacy, building uses were stacked vertically. The retail area, which occupies the lower four levels, provides direct access from street level and circulation by escalators to all shops. The office section is on the second through eleventh floors, and the hotel, its banquet rooms, and Founders restaurant occupy the top seven floors.

A significant design feature is the new six-floor atrium, which soars from the twelfth to the eighteenth floor. Filled with natural light from four enormous skylights, the atrium evokes the atmosphere of a European-style courtyard.

Listed on the National Register of Historic Places, this was one of the most luxurious hotels in America when it opened in 1904. Working in association with the Vitetta Group/Studio Four, great care was taken to preserve its French Renaissance Revival architecture.

1

1   Renovated facade
2   Main lobby
3   The Conservatory Restaurant
4   Hotel entrance
5   The new retail component

2

3

4

5

Wyndham Hotel at Playhouse Square

Design/Completion 1993/1995
Cleveland, Ohio
Wyndham Hotels and Resorts and
Playhouse Square Foundation
205-room urban hotel
Steel construction clad in pre-cast concrete panels

RTKL's design positions the hotel along downtown Cleveland's main boulevard, Euclid Avenue, on a prominent triangular site that marks the beginning of the Playhouse Square District, an area of four historic theaters that is on the National Register of Historic Places. It houses three levels of public spaces, along with 10 levels of guestrooms. The lobby, Winsor's, a 75-seat restaurant and 35-seat bar, and guest registration areas are located on the first floor. The grand ballroom and meeting rooms are located on the second and third floor. An indoor swimming pool and health club are located in the basement.

The hotel's exterior design takes architectural elements from the surrounding historic buildings and reinterprets them in a more contemporary manner, while still respecting the proportions and materials of context. In particular, the lower two stories of the building are richly architectural to preserve the concept of storefront and urban continuity that is important along the main street of Euclid Avenue. The cylinder at the prow of the site not only helps turn the corner, but also represents a new beacon for the newly revitalized Playhouse Square District.

1

1   Main elevation
2   Typical guestroom floor plan
3   Lobby plan
4   Tower detail
5   Lobby bar

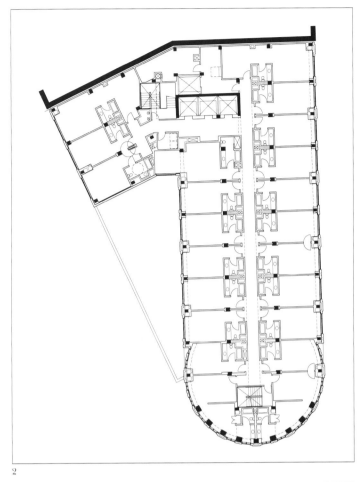

2

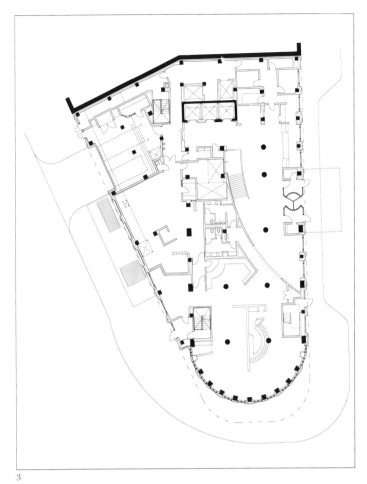

3

4

5

Leisure/
Entertainment

China Gate

Design 1995
Inchon Song-Do, Korea
Confidential
Steel frame
Stone and metal exterior cladding and glazed curtain wall

China Gate is the centerpiece of an extensive mixed-use development of recreation and entertainment venues being planned for the Song-Do Resort District. The project contains a cultural center with rides, sports, shows and events, as well as retail and food venues.

This synergy of combined uses creates a dynamic, leisure-based environment, conceived as a journey and adventure of discovery. This notion is reflected in the network of circulation, changes in elevation, and spatial organization, all of which lead visitors through a variety of overlapping paths and spaces.

1

2

1　Overall model view
2　Model view
3　Exhibition pavilion
4&5　Site section

3

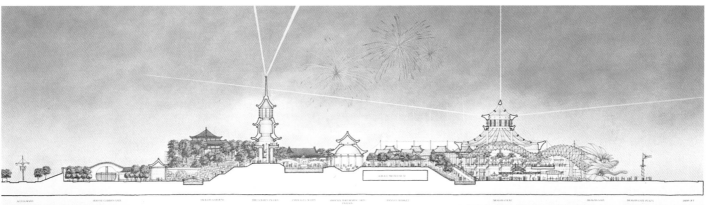

4

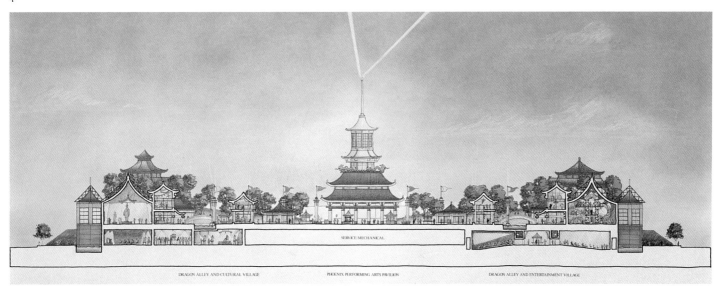

DRAGON ALLEY AND CULTURAL VILLAGE　　PHOENIX PERFORMING ARTS PAVILION　　DRAGON ALLEY AND ENTERTAINMENT VILLAGE

5

Reston Pavilion

Design/Completion 1992/1993
Reston, Virginia
Reston Town Center Associates
6,000 square feet
Steel and aluminum frame construction
Glass panels and poured concrete foundation

An open-air pavilion completes Phase One of Reston Town Center, the mixed-use urban core of a suburban Washington, DC, planned community. Located at the edge of the town square along the main thoroughfare, the pavilion is used for ice skating in the winter and for concerts, festivals, receptions, and other events during the warmer months.

Forty-four feet in height, the pavilion consists of a permanent ice rink; exposed steel, glass, and aluminum structure; and a cantilevered skylit roof. The pavilion's structure and form are evocative of 19th century European exposition hall architecture. Metal elements also whimsically allude to the blades of ice skates.

A fabric and aluminum track system creates a tight tent-like enclosure that can be raised and lowered easily during changing weather conditions. The pavilion also incorporates retractable sun and acoustic shades.

Both as a sculptural object in space and a focal point for the activities enjoyed there, the award-winning pavilion helps create a memorable urban vitality.

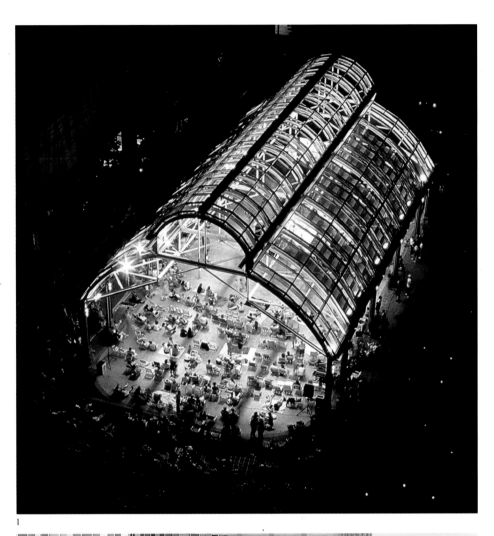

1

2

1 Night shot
2 View from the north
3–8 Details

3

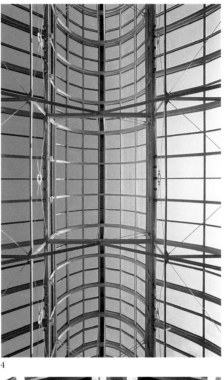

4

5

6

7

8

Universal Studios Hollywood Starway and Backlot Tram Tour Facility

Design/Completion 1991/1995
Los Angeles, California
MCA/Universal Studios
900-foot moving walkway and 6,800-square-foot tram facility
Two-toned cement, cast-stone, stainless steel, green glass,
canvas, and brick paving

As with any entertainment-based development, the movement and control of people is critical. RTKL's involvement in the expansion and upgrade of the 350-acre MCA/Universal Studio Tour has involved two major people-moving elements.

A signature feature of the tour is the "Starway," one of the world's largest escalator systems. Linking the theme park on the upper level with the motion picture studio on the lower level, four banks of escalators cascade down a steep hillside. A glass canopy and light show visible for thirty miles enhance the system which is capable of moving 8,000 people per hour.

Making room for future expansion, the Backlot Tram Tour Facility was re-designed and re-located. The new facility and its adjacent boarding area accommodate trams at the rate of 23 per hour, with each tram carrying 150 people. An elevator or glass canopied escalator, smaller in scale but similar to the Starway, transports visitors from a plaza down to the tram boarding area.

1

2

1 The Starway at night
2 Aerial view of tramway boarding facility
3&4 Starway escalator
5 Backlot tram entry marquee

3

4

5

The Trocadero

Design/Completion 1994/1996
London, England
Burford Group plc
475,000 square feet in interconnected multi-building complex
Steel structure with historic Portland stone facades
Interior metal work with encased columns, video monitors and
large-scale project screens

For the refurbishment of this historic development in Piccadilly Circus, RTKL have transformed The Trocadero into a next-wave leisure destination—home to Europe's first SegaWorld, a 100,000-square-foot virtual reality theme park.

Using storyboard techniques, RTKL choreographed a series of experiences that integrate architectural themeing, graphics, lighting and audio-visual technology. An existing three-level atrium has been opened the entire height of the building, and a dramatic vertical transportation network created. Visitors are greeted by a portal that leads to a mid-level platform surrounded by a 200+ monitor videowall. From here, visitors climb aboard the rocket-shot escalator that takes them to the theme park's entry.

Throughout, the intention is to control the environment completely and create a series of events that culminates in a staged event, a multi-media extravaganza that will encompass film and theater played out on the videowall and reinforced by state-of-the-art audio-visual, lasers and lighting effects.

1

2

3

4

1   View of refurbished atrium
2–4   The T-roc character
5   Multi-media tower
6   Building section
7   View from the east of existing building
8   The rocket-shot escalator

5

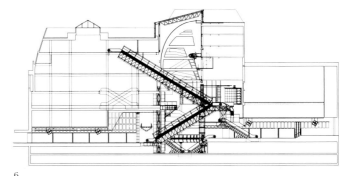

6

7

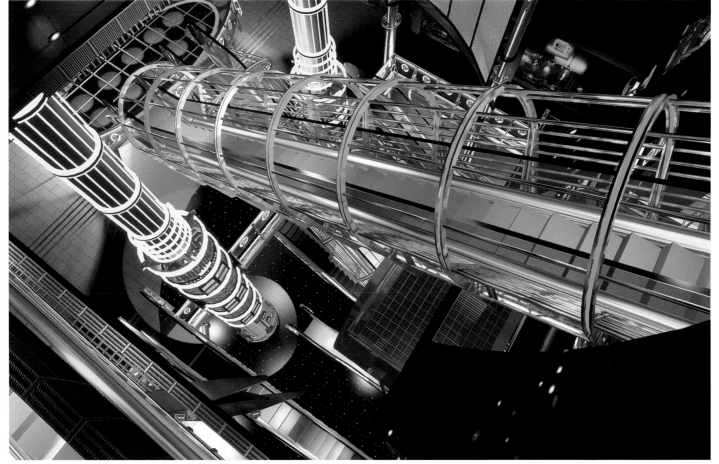

8

Port Orleans and Dixie Landings

Design/Completion 1989/1990
Orlando, Florida
Disney Development Company

Disney's Dixie Landings and Port Orleans resorts are located northeast of EPCOT Center on the Walt Disney World property in Florida. A navigable waterway threads through the 3,000-room project, serving as a significant amenity and major source of transportation.

To help reinforce the "American South" theme throughout the resort, RTKL provided full graphic design services (from schematic design through construction administration) for all feature signage, directional and decorative signage, logo design, and print graphics.

Colorful graphics for Port Orleans express the jazz and architectural influences of New Orleans and its historic French Quarter, while the more rural Dixie Landings is reflected by Southern folk art and plantation and bayou imagery such as paddleboats, alligators, and magnolia trees.

1

1   Entry sign
2   Mardi Gras Parade
3   Project identity
4   Transom grille
5   Icon sign
6   Way-finding graphics
7   Poolside bar sign

2

3

4

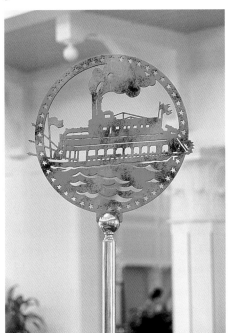

5

6

7

The Entertainment Center at Irvine Spectrum

Design/Completion 1994/1995
Irvine, California
The Irvine Company
New 270,000 square feet
Brick and masonry

Combining leisure and retail uses to create a unique commercial destination for the Southern California market, The Entertainment Center capitalizes on its location at the intersection of two major freeways to draw visitors and shoppers from the entire Los Angeles metropolitan area.

The plan has been organized around a central plaza to create a vibrant, animated space. The 270,000-square foot Center integrates a two-one screen Edward's Cinema multiplex and 110,000 square feet of retail and entertainment, including themed restaurants and the Oasis food court with seating for 400 people.

The design playfully recalls Moroccan-style Mediterranean architecture and art—its open-air plaza, recurring domes and a central gazebo are complemented by bright, imaginative environmental graphics. Public spaces are kept large nearer the cinema and gently transition into narrower, more traditional passageways. Bold patterns and streamlined elements are used to outline gathering areas and draw people to the heart of the Center.

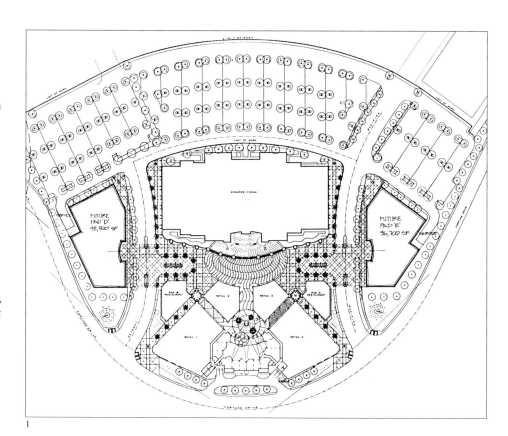

1

2

1   Site plan
2   Central courtyard
3   Paving medallion
4   Central courtyard
5–7   Environmental graphic detail

3

5

4

6

7

Office Buildings

Charles Center South

Design/Completion 1973/1975
Baltimore, Maryland
Area 16B Associates, Inc.
25-story, 300,000-square foot office tower
Steel structure sheathed in tinted curtain wall

Located on a prominent corner at the southern tip of Charles Center, the area in the heart of Baltimore that sparked its heralded urban renaissance, this RTKL-designed office building was selected through a design competition. Its six-sided, prismatic configuration tempers the angularity of the site and presents a multi-faceted profile toward the city.

Rising from a granite base, the tower is completely sheathed in solar gray glass panels, studded with stainless steel buttons. In its polished simplicity, the design makes a strong statement without overshadowing its neighbors, smoothing the transition between Charles Center and the Inner Harbor to the south.

1

2

1   View from Pratt Street
2   Main entry

Federated Building

Design/Completion 1977/1978
Cincinnati, Ohio
Federated Department Stores, Inc.
21-story, 350,000-square foot
Steel structure

This landmark corporate headquarters building, home of Federated Department Stores, was designed by RTKL and built by the Henry C. Beck Company, a team selected by means of a national design/build competition.

Design challenges were posed by the necessity of building over an existing parking garage which was used to support new construction. In addition, desirable views across the Ohio River were partially blocked by tall structures directly south of the building. The design solution is a triangular tower with slanting sides that face southeast and southwest, focusing views around adjacent buildings toward the river.

1

2

1   View from the west
2   Beveled elevation

Block 68 Competition

Design 1995
Beirut, Lebanon
Solidere
Concrete
Local stone and curtain wall cladding

Block 68, positioned at the edge of both the old French Quarter and the location of the new Souks, embodies the tension between old and new, forming an urbanistic transition point between districts. RTKL's competition entry attempts to reconcile this transition, seemlessly re-weaving the urban fabric of the old city with the plan of a future Beirut.

The building has been conceived as a series of layers or tiers, blending the palette and vocabulary of the city's past with that of today's modern office building. The facades, envisioned as local stone, retain the proportions of the historic facades along Al Maarad, continuing the ABAABA rhythm established by the adjacent building. Sculpturally, the building is comprised of an assemblage of tall vertical masses that reflect the character and proportion of the 1970s adjacent building and the building proposed for the corner opposite.

The building has been designed with flexible floorplates and is capable of accommodating the latest in office building technology and building systems.

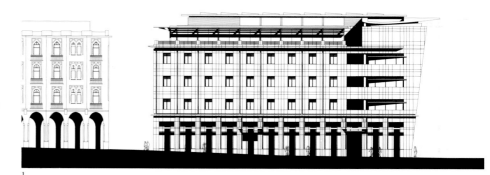

1

2

1   Elevation with partial view of old building
2   View from Rue Weygand

140

Gentor Oficinas Corporativas

Design 1993
Monterrey, Mexico
Grupo Gentor
50,000 square feet
Cast-in-place concrete clad in Burlington stone and sandstone

Capturing the dramatic razorback mountain views of Garza Garcia in Monterrey, Mexico, RTKL has organized the headquarters of the Gentor Corporation into four distinct zones, with the president's suite, vice presidents' suites, executive offices on level 1 and 2, and support staff and ancillary spaces housed on the lower (at grade) level.

In response to the client's desire for a low building, the architect has taken advantage of the site's slope and interweaves office spaces and landscape elements, with each workstation or office enjoying natural light and direct access to terraces or outdoor gardens. In addition, cascading water elements provide both visual and audio excitement throughout the project.

The building is designed to be discovered gradually, as an element within the landscape; visitors approach from above, past the guardhouse and a series of three grass pyramids set atop a paved, palm tree court framed by pergolas.

1

2

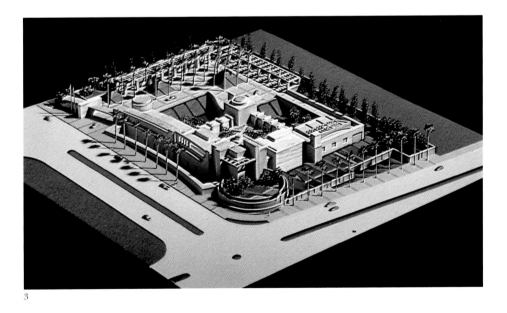

3

1&2   Elevations
  3   Model view

Warsaw Business Center

Design/Completion 1995/1998
Warsaw, Poland
Daewoo Corporation
Planning and architecture for 50,000-square-meter,
40-story tower with office, retail, and restaurants

With their expanding role in the Eastern European market, the Daewoo Corporation commissioned RTKL to design this new headquarters as a landmark in the city of Warsaw. Grand in demeanour, yet efficient in design and materials, the project comprises office space as well as retail, restaurants, a health club, and a large wintergarden atrium.

Facing the street entrance, the wintergarden doubles as a showcase for Daewoo's latest advances in automobile technology as well as their entire line of electronics products.

Among the building's sustainable design features are solar orientations which have been used to maximum advantage as well as a selection of indigenous plants and plantings that require low maintenance.

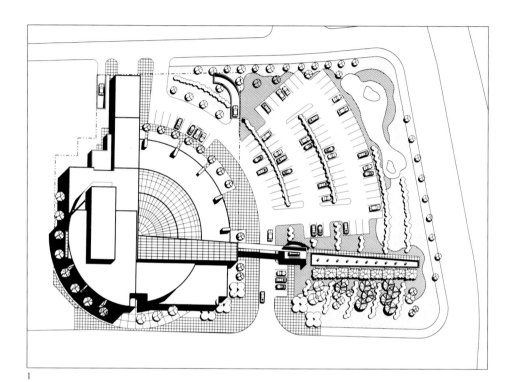

1

2

142

1   Site plan
2   Concept sketches
3&4   Model views
5   Concept diagrams

3

4

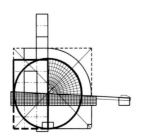

5

Shanghai Business Center

Design/Completion 1995/1998
Shanghai, China
Confidential
135,000 square meters of office space; 40,000 square meters of retail; 500-room business hotel; 1000 apartments

Organized around a large central plaza, this 416,000-square-meter multi-use development answers the client's desire for a landmark project. The design boldly incorporates an 89-story office tower that cuts a prominent silhouette on the Shanghai skyline.

As the large plaza in the foreground draws people in, a retail corridor visually connects the project with adjacent commercial development and lends a pedestrian scale to the project at street level. To reach the retail element, shoppers and visitors pass through a glass-enclosed wintergarden.

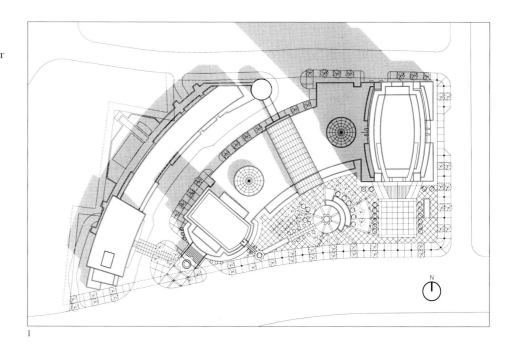

1

1   Site plan
2   Model view

2

144

Sui Bao Tower

Design/Completion 1995/1998
Shenzhen, China
Shirble Holdings Ltd
90,000 square meters
Structural steel
Polished stone cladding and articulated
aluminum mullions

This new headquarters office tower is
located in downtown Shenzhen, an hour
from the island of Hong Kong.

Envisioned as a strong visual symbol for
Shirble Holdings Ltd, the building is
conceived as a classic skyscraper,
emphasizing its height by its slenderness.
The 90,000-square-meter mixed-use
project will also include apartments and a
retail base.

1

1   Artist's perspective

Centro Empresarial Monterrey

Design/Completion 1991/1998
Monterrey, Mexico
ICA Asociadas
30 stories, 370,000 square feet
Steel
Curtain wall and stone finishes

RTKL's design concept for the Centro Empresarial Monterrey tower responds to two primary goals: the creation of a strong visual symbol for the city, and the development of a building that is appropriate to its historic and geographic context.

Conceived as a classic skyscraper, the tower's slenderness emphasizes its height, while its stepped crown creates a dynamic profile. Positioned to capture views of the city and Sierra Madre the building relates well to both the scale and massing of other buildings on downtown Monterrey's Macro Plaza.

The interior layout provides a variety of tenant spaces within three basic floor plates. The lower floors provide the largest contiguous spaces, bisected by the building lobby and offering direct views of the street and plaza. Mid-level floors can be divided into tenant spaces, many offering two-level atriums and outdoor terraces. High-rise floors offer more efficient perimeter office layouts, optimum leasing depths, and internal connections for multi-level tenants.

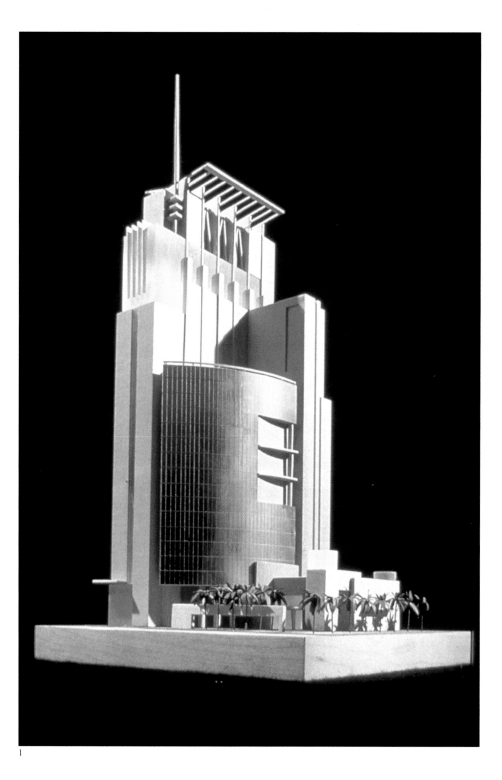

1

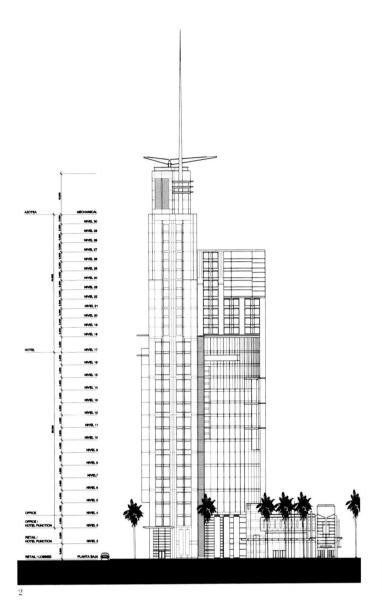

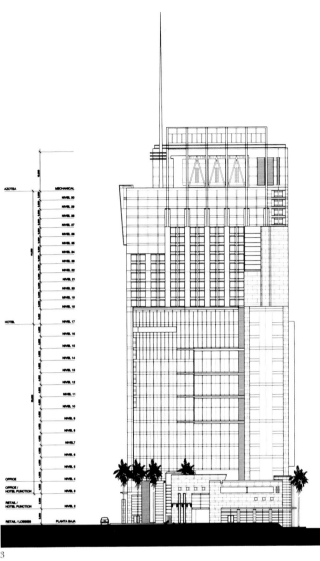

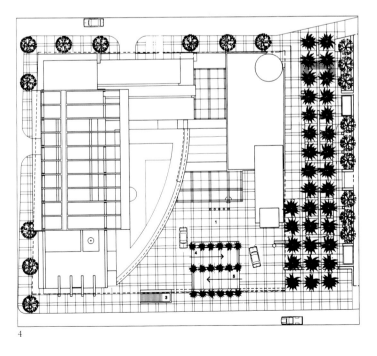

1 Model view
2 East elevation
3 South elevation
4 Site plan

Commerce Place

Design/Completion 1989/1993
Baltimore, Maryland
Harlan-KDC Associates
720,000 square feet, 30 stories
Exposed aggregate pre-cast panels poured concrete structure

RTKL designed and engineered Commerce Place, a 30-story Class A office tower in Baltimore's expanding financial and municipal district, to respond sensitively to its urban context.

Commerce Place recalls the classical forms of early 20th century skyscrapers with its clearly articulated base, middle, and top and richly detailed glass and masonry skin. Outdoor terraces and setbacks at each tower elevation create visual interest and diversity. At ground level, the main entrance features a glass-enclosed vaulted lobby.

RTKL also designed Redwood Court, an urban park adjacent to the building, as a quiet oasis in the middle of downtown. Portions of the elaborate facade of the Mercantile Safe Deposit and Trust Building, the site's former occupant, were preserved and incorporated as a significant element of the park design.

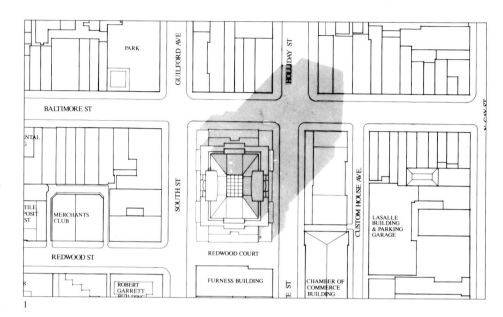

1

2

148

1   Site plan
2   View from the east
3   View from Gay Street

3

Fairfax County Government Center

Design/Completion 1989/1992
Fairfax County, Virginia
The Smith/Artery Partnership
675,000 square feet
Poured concrete construction
Reflective glass facade with granite on pre-cast panels

Located on a scenic 100-acre site outside Washington, DC, the Fairfax County Government Center consolidates many of the county's government departments in an elliptical six-story building. RTKL's design was the winning entry in an invited developer competition, and the project was developed through a creative public/private partnership between Fairfax County and private developers.

The public forum area at the entrance serves as lobby, gallery, and meeting area, finished with natural stone surfaces and wood veneers and a combination of natural stone and carpeting for the flooring. Underground parking for 1,076 cars is provided on two levels.

A phased construction schedule allowed the completed south end of the building to proceed with county fit-up and furniture installation while construction continued on the north end of the base building.

With the capacity to expand to one million square feet, this outstanding government center will be the focus of a new 3.1 million-square-foot development area west of the city of Fairfax.

1

2

1   Aerial view
2   Main meeting room
3   Public forum
4   Main entry
5   Main approach

3

4

5

The Marsh & McLennan Building

Design/Completion 1987/1989
Baltimore, Maryland
Stone & Associates, Inc.
77,000 square feet
Historic cast iron facade and an addition of steel brise-soleil
with curtain wall

RTKL's adaptive use of one of Baltimore's last remaining cast iron buildings integrates new construction with the restoration of an historic landmark. Constructed in 1871 as an office and warehouse for the Wilkens Brush Company, the original five-story, six-bay building is listed on the National Register of Historic Places and exhibits a degree of ornamentation relatively rare in cast iron structures.

RTKL's design goal was to create a unified architectural statement without exaggerating the original or new building elements. The uncompromisingly modern five-story addition extends and envelopes the cast iron building, retaining the scale and texture of both facades in perfect harmony. A brise-soleil across the main south elevation reinterprets the texture, depth, and detailing of the original cast iron facade and enhances the energy efficiency of the building.

Additional preservation and restoration work (performed to National Park Service standards) included the complete inventory and restoration of the cast iron facade, wood windows and storefront doors, and an interior stair.

1

1 Cast iron facade with new addition
2 View from entry plaza
3 Side illustration
4 View from Pratt Street

2

3

4

Headquarters Facility

Design/Completion 1995/1998
Virginia
General Services Administration
24,000 square meters
Cast-in-place concrete
Brick, pre-cast panel and glass facade

Located on a wooded site, this new Headquarters Facility takes advantage of spectacular views of the surrounding landscape. Integrating the building into a dramatic hilltop site, and carefully accommodating both secure and non-secure areas, RTKL's design includes office, laboratory, computer, and communications space, an auditorium, cafeteria, fitness center, and daycare center.

Design goals for the project include the creation of a productive work environment within a highly secure protocol and expression of the client's advanced technology focus, within the rich architectural vernacular of the local region.

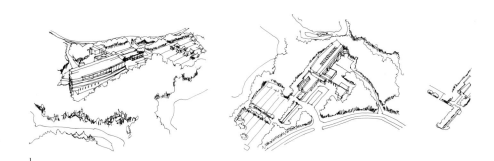

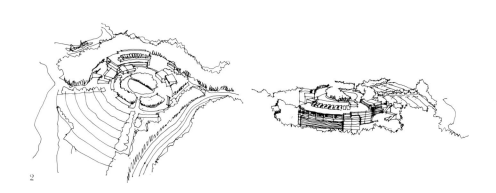

1 Concept sketch, scheme A
2 Concept sketch, scheme B
3 Model view, scheme B

SABIC Headquarters

Design 1995
Riyadh, Saudi Arabia
Saudi Arabian Basic Industries Corporation
Associate Architect: Saudi Diyar
Concrete
Riyadh stone-clad facade and wood trellises

RTKL's competition entry for SABIC's new headquarters is a campus of interconnected buildings in line with the north/south grid of the city of Riyadh. Two strong fortress-like walls offer protection against the sun and desert, and create a clear distinction amongst uses—public space to the west; service and "back-of-house" to the east. Between the walls, the space is subdivided by three connecting spans at the first level which create a series of protected inner courts.

The western wall encloses the public "street," a re-interpretation of the souk, where public activities (cafeterias, library, meeting and training rooms) are located. Many of these look out onto the inner courtyards between the walls and some, notably the cafeteria and VIP dining room, are positioned as jewel-like pavilions with views of the landscaped gardens.

At the southern end, a dramatic cylindrical volume serves as the main reception area and houses the SABIC exhibition center. At the northern end of the "street" is the auditorium, the public meeting place, that opens out to an amphitheater for open-air presentations during the cooler months.

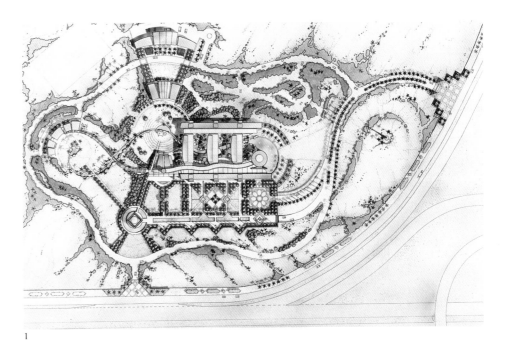

1

2

1   Illustrative site plan
2   Aerial view

Sudirman Tower

Design/Completion 1991/1995
Jakarta, Indonesia
Lippoland Development
Associate Architect: PT Airmas Asri
200,000 square feet on 20 stories
Steel
Polished granite and glass cladding

RTKL provided architectural design services for Lippo Bank's 20-story headquarters office tower located in the southern tip of Jakarta's "Golden Triangle" commercial zone.

The tower is a memorable image against the urban skyline. A three-story combined office lobby/banking chamber will serve as a monumental entry leading visitors and workers to 200,000 square feet of leasable space. Restaurants on the 19th and 20th floors will feature 360-degree views of the city and provide a glow to the tower penthouse at night.

1

1   Main lobby
2   Main lobby and reception
3   Site plan
4   View from JL Jend Sudirman

2

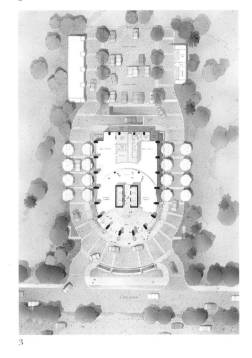

3

4

TNB Corporate Tower

Design 1995
Kuala Lumpur, Malaysia
Tanaga Nasional Berhad
Executive Architect: GDP Architects SDN BHD
60 stories
Steel frame
Office tower: glass, metal panel cladding and brise soleil
Service tower: perforated metal skin cladding

RTKL and GDP designed this competition entry for this headquarters office tower to symbolize the strength of Kuala Lumpur's electric company and the energy of the rapidly emerging Malaysian economy. The transmission of light, power, and electricity, and the evocation of the country's rich cultural heritage, combine to be the guiding forces of the design.

The design includes two major components: a 60-story glass and stainless steel tower with eye-shaped floor plates and a connected 80-story, star-shaped service tower clad with metal screen. The service tower is internally illuminated, creating a nightly beacon and a bold expression of light and energy.

The two vertical masses create a dynamic tension between opposing elements and materials—dark juxtaposed with light, solid against fluid, and metal against glass.

The tower is located at the edge of a newly masterplanned corporate campus and gestures strongly toward the street capitalizing on views of the city skyline.

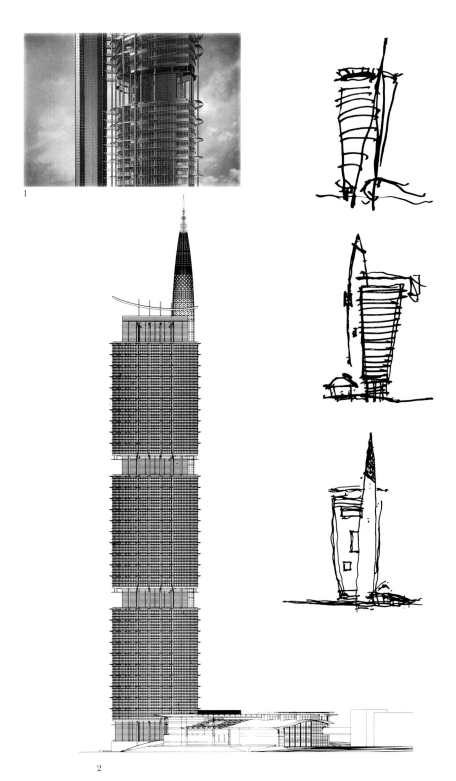

1

2

1   Tower detail
2   East elevation
3   Overall view

3

Beijing Bao Xin International Financial Centre

Design/Completion 1995/1999
Beijing, China
China National Insurance Trust & Investment Co.
Associate Architect and Engineers: Building Design Institute of the Ministry of Construction
Joint Venture Partner: Bennett & Wright International, Toronto/Beijing
1.3 million-square-foot tower
Exterior of granite stone veneer, stainless steel clad with insulating glass; steel and aluminum louvers, vents, grilles, and screens

Creating a strong signature on the Beijing skyline, RTKL has designed the headquarters of the investment arm of China's only insurance company as a 22-level tower atop a five-level commercial podium.

Located prominently in the city's emerging financial district, the building is conceived as two dominant masses, each creating a strong edge to the street. A bold central tower holds the corner and marks the building's main entry, welcoming visitors into a five-story lobby.

The building forms an enclosed courtyard to the rear, where a skylit wintergarden mirrors the shape of the cylindrical tower. Providing vertical and horizontal access to the retail podium, the wintergarden serves also as gradual transition to the courtyard's green spaces—a natural buffer that lies between the tower and nearby buildings.

The building also includes a business center, health club, and restaurants. Parking for nearly 1,800 bicycles and 370 automobiles is located below grade.

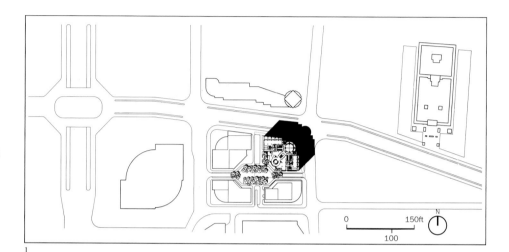

1

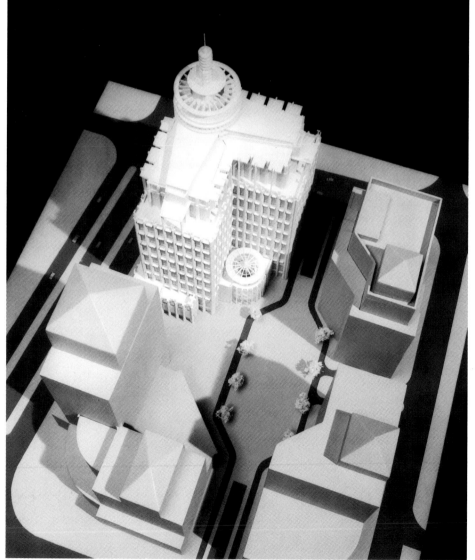

2

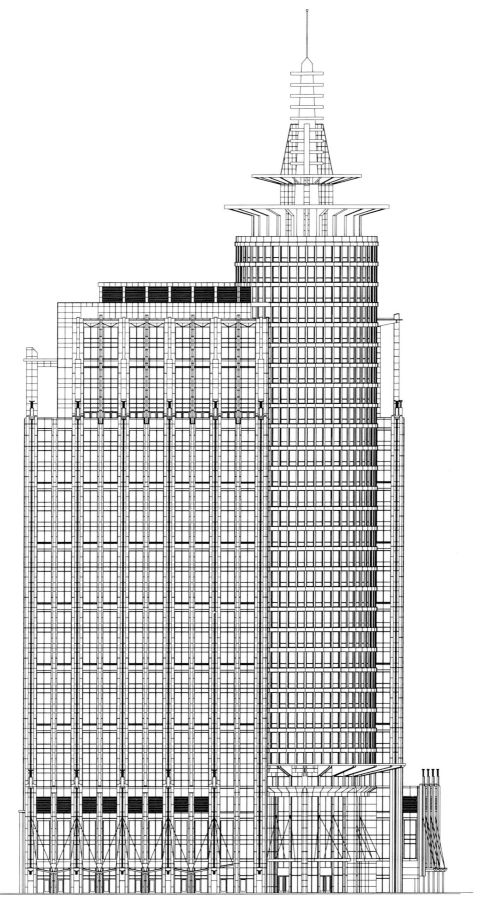

3

Health Sciences

Rebecca M. Clatanoff Women's Hospital, Anne Arundel Medical Center

Design/Completion 1992/1995
Annapolis, Maryland
Anne Arundel Medical Center
114,000-square-foot Women's Hospital; 82,000-square-foot
Medical Office Building
Steel
Combination of brick, cut stone and concrete masonry units
accentuated by bay windows of glass and aluminum curtain wall

Phase II of an RTKL-masterplanned campus, the Rebecca M. Clatanoff Women's Hospital completes a U-shaped building configuration begun with the ambulatory surgery center and an oncology treatment center. The plan's composition and scale create the atmosphere of an urban space, as each building's primary entrance faces the courtyard.

Linked to the ambulatory surgery center, Level One of the hospital contains facilities for Reception, Admitting, Imaging, Laboratory, and Pre-Admission Testing as well as a new dining area that serves the entire campus.

Level Two contains 22 private LDRP rooms, 14 private surgical nursing rooms, facilities for C-Section and delivery, and a Level Two Nursery. A central atrium brings natural light and views to all areas of this level.

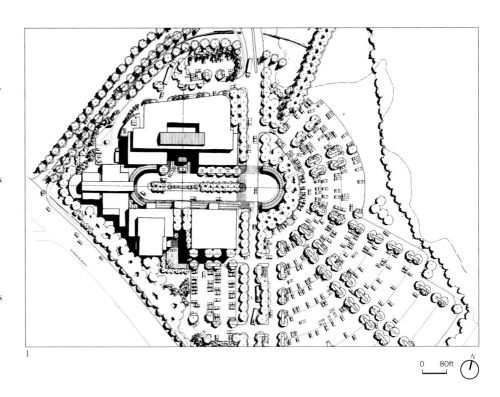

1

0   80ft

2

1 Site plan
2 Main entry, Women's Hospital
3 Entry foyer
4 Cafeteria
5 Nurse's station
6 Labor and delivery room

3

4

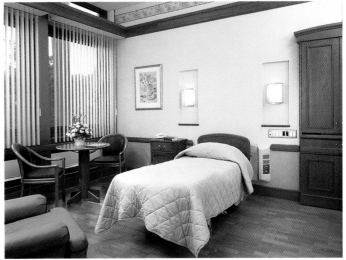

5

6

Johns Hopkins Bayview Medical Center, Francis Scott Key Pavilion

Design/Completion 1991/1994
Baltimore, Maryland
Johns Hopkins Bayview Medical Center
297,000 square feet
Three story pre-cast concrete base with brick clad patient floors
Glass and metal curtain wall system with warm-gray pre-cast concrete and terra cotta-colored brick as exterior materials

The Francis Scott Key Pavilion is an acute patient tower addition and partial renovation of the original 1930s Baltimore City Hospital that serves as the Johns Hopkins Bayview Medical Center's "flagship" facility.

To allow expansion capabilities and keep campus traditions of balancing public and private indoor and outdoor spaces, a "main street" with a prominent public waiting area was introduced to serve as a consistent orientation element. Acting as a seam, the main street marries the existing building to the varying floors of the addition and instills a clear circulation system in a building type renowned for the contrary.

As the Pavilion is the focus of the campus, the tower's vertical circulation core becomes the focus of the building form. The core divides public/outpatient circulation from service/inpatient circulation on each level. Each departmental unit originates from the core circulation system, providing a consistent organizational structure at each level and a resultant clarity of circulation patterns. The disposition of functions within the building base allows horizontal expansion to both east and west.

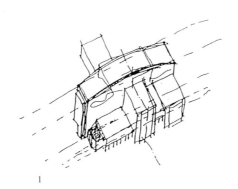

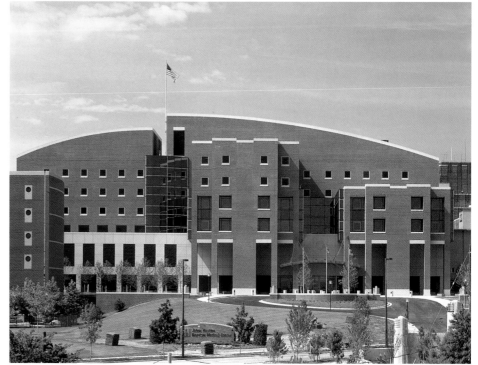

1   Concept sketch
2   Entry detail
3   Main entry

Summerlin Medical Center and Facilities Site Masterplanning

Design/Completion 1995/1996
Las Vegas, Nevada
Universal Health Services Inc.
407,000 square feet
Pre-cast concrete forms with glass and metal panel planes
Base of red sandstone retaining walls and freestanding columns

RTKL has designed this multi-use medical facility to be built in four phases. The initial phase includes a medical office building, diagnostic and surgical center, and a cancer treatment center. Subsequent phases include an acute care hospital, sub-acute (skilled nursing) facility, and additional medical offices and outpatient facilities.

The design of the medical office building has been conceived as three separate masses. These forms, unified by glass and metal panel planes, rest on red sandstone retaining walls and freestanding columns. One mass anchors the building toward the outpatient clinic, the second contains the core and stair towers, while the third appears to float above the main entry terrace, canting dynamically toward Town Center Drive. Metal sunscreens shade the large glazed areas separating the pre-cast concrete forms articulated by deeply punched windows.

The diagnostic and surgical center and the cancer treatment center repeat the same vocabulary, utilizing the sandstone base to anchor the masses above.

1

2

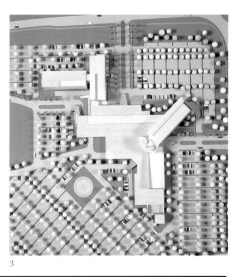

3

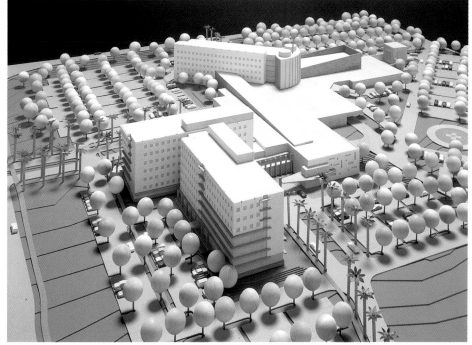

4

1&2   Concept sketches
3&4   Model views

The Johns Hopkins Hospital Redevelopment

Design/Completion 1973/1983
Baltimore, Maryland
The Johns Hopkins Hospital
60-acre urban campus

RTKL has enjoyed a long and successful history with The Johns Hopkins Hospital, one of the most highly regarded medical institutions in the world. As the master plan and design architects for the redevelopment of the hospital, RTKL worked in close co-operation with administrative and medical staff in defining long-range program needs, evaluating existing facilities, designing a total development program, and developing detailed architectural programs for all new and renovated facilities on the campus. Existing facilities ranged in age from 20 to 100 years and the medical program requirements touched virtually every clinical and support department of the hospital.

The redevelopment effort provided the hospital with nearly one million square feet of new space, 260,000 square feet of renovated space, 418 new patient beds, 277 renovated patient beds, 2,600 additional parking spaces, and new utility, transportation, and circulation systems.

1

1   The Nelson-Harvey building and the historic Houck building
2   Aerial view with the Marburg building in the foreground
3   Public space
4   Main entrance

2

3

4

Greater Baltimore Medical Center, Obstetrics/Acute Care Expansion & Renovation

Design/Completion 1988/1993 (Phase I)
Design/Completion 1990/1993 (Phase II)
Baltimore, Maryland
Greater Baltimore Medical Center
180,000 square feet addition; 100,000 square feet renovation
Steel structural frame with wire-cut brick and pre-cast concrete selected to match the original 1964 building; teak stressed wood is used to create pedestrian-scaled entrance canopies for the new and existing building, recalling the teak exterior soffits of the original building

The Obstetrics/Acute Care project is the first major expansion of Greater Baltimore Medical Center since the hospital was originally designed by RTKL in 1964.

The multi-phase project consists of a six-level addition, the primary focus of which is the Women's Center, offering a full complement of obstetrics, labor, delivery and recovery services. The acute levels above include departments of surgery, medicine, and cardiology; coronary, medical, and surgical intensive care units; nursing units; and related support facilities.

The addition has been designed to respect the character of GBMC's campus setting and mature site. Walkways and balconies surround the new enclosed courtyard, maximizing natural light and views of the surrounding wooded hillside. The extensive use of wood and brick adds richness and warmth to the public spaces. Special paving textures and landscaping define circulation and parking areas, while a man-made wildlife pond and new gate house enhance GBMC's entry drive.

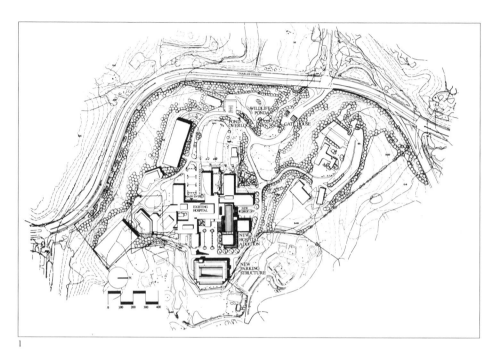

1

2

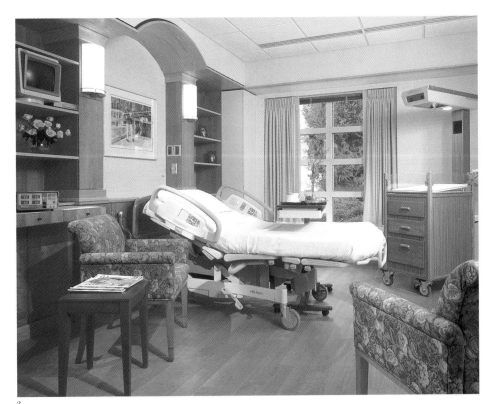

3

1   Site plan
2   Building detail
3   Patient room
4   Main entry

4

Miscellaneous

US Ambassador's Residence, Tokyo, Japan

Design/Completion 1992/1995
Tokyo, Japan
US Department of State, Office of Foreign Buildings Operations
37,000 square foot existing building (c. 1931) on a 1.4-acre site

RTKL provided architecture, engineering, and interior architecture services for the renovation and restoration of the Tokyo Embassy Main Residence (EMR). The residence has been restored to its original architectural character with all building systems brought up to contemporary standards.

The first ambassador's residence built expressly for that purpose by the United States government, the "California Deco" building exhibits a rare combination of early 20th-century styles.

Based on RTKL's thorough on-site building evaluation and report, the scope of work included complete rehabilitation of the residence, including all exterior and interior finishes, roofing, electrical and mechanical systems, kitchen remodeling, and renovation of perimeter walls, structures, and landscaping. New construction encompasses a glass entrance canopy and additional public restrooms.

1

1 Main lobby
2 External view
3 Drawing room
4 Entrance hall

2

3

4

US Ambassador's Residence, Bayan, Kuwait

Design/Completion 1995/1996
Bayan, Kuwait
US Department of State, Office of Foreign Building Operations
1,000 square meters
Concrete
Veneer Roman brick on the lower floors and synthetic stucco plaster
on the upper floors; extensive wood verandahs and balconies

Because the ambassador's residence is located on the main embassy compound, RTKL was charged to create a design that was compatible with the existing structures while evoking a feeling of residential retreat. The architecture reflects a mix of American house planning and vernacular Islamic architectural themes; and the use of landscaping and fenestration emphasize residence over office.

The western elevation, which is along the most trafficked street, is characterized by two-story-high verandahs and exaggerated mechanical penthouses. These serve to give the residence an "address" different from the rest of the compound.

Color and materials are compatible with the rest of the compound. Half-barrel vaults over the representational portions of the house give the residence a form unique to the rest of the compound and thus reinforce the difference in use.

1

2

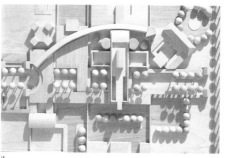

3

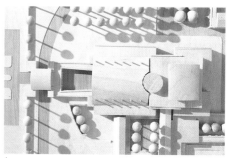

4

1   Elevation
2   Building perspective
3&4   Model details/alternative designs

176

Sculpture Studio

Design/Completion 1989/1990
(Dismantled 1991)
Baltimore, Maryland
Maryland Institute, College of Art
2,000 square feet
Wood (telephone pole) and cable
Corrugated steel and fiberglass panel construction

A temporary studio designed pro bono by RTKL provided work space for three Japanese artists to construct a 3-ton wood sculpture of a Buddha. Widely published in the design press, the project received a 1991 AIA Honor Award, the profession's highest recognition of design excellence for individual buildings, and a 1990 design award from the Baltimore Chapter/AIA.

Located at the Maryland Institute, College of Art, the 55-foot-high studio is 40 feet wide and 50 feet long, large enough to house raw materials, tools, and the completed 33-foot-high sculpture. The design reflects a Japanese simplicity in its emphasis on natural light and the use of color and common building materials. Corrugated steel, prefabricated fiberglass building panels (which take on a rice-paper quality), and telephone poles all met the client's requirements for inexpensive, reusable, and easily assembled/disassembled materials.

During the summer, the studio's fiberglass panels can swing open for ventilation and to allow visitors to watch the artists at work.

1

2

1   Section
2   Exterior view

Miyazaki Station

Design/Completion 1989/1993
Miyazaki City, Miyazaki Prefecture, Japan
JR Kyushu
97,000 square feet
Associate Architect: Seibu Kotsu Architectural Office
Steel
Perforated metal panels, cabling and framework

The design for Miyazaki Station takes its cue from the simple elegance of a Japanese lantern. The building creates a focal point on axis to Nation Road 10, the city's major thoroughfare, and defines a large civic space. The delicacy of the elements allows the structure to be grand in scale without being massive in form.

The bold entry tower, the protruding elevation, the plan angle and the recognition of the major street axis combine to provide a clear and dramatic entry sequence. The fluidity of the linear elevation is created through repetition of forms and elements, as though each bay were the car of a train. The towers provide verticality and balance to the continuous horizontal space frame wall, while the wave canopy emphasizes movement across the face of the building and creates a more intimate, human-scale element at the building facade.

1

2

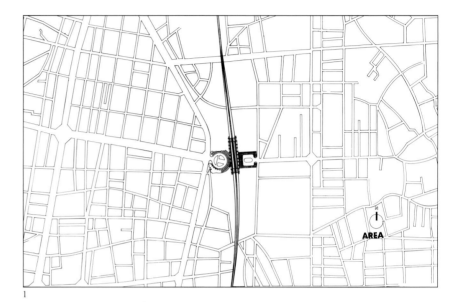

3

1 Site plan
2 Platform kiosk
3 Aerial view of West Plaza
4 West station entry

4

Embassy of Singapore

Design/Completion 1990/1993
Washington, DC
Republic of Singapore
55,000 square feet
Concrete frame
Brick facade and stone trim

Located on a prominent corner site at the gateway to Washington's new embassy district, this new embassy combines building form and landscape to express Singapore's image as a lush garden city and a growing, progressive country.

The design fuses geometry—a cruciform represents the past while a circle symbolizes the future—with nature. The initial approach to the embassy is marked by a large garden, framed by two sides of the building and a curved wall. A materials palette derived from Singapore's black-and-white houses, teak-louvered windows, and large overhanging roofs conveys the Republic's vernacular architecture.

The embassy's first two floors house consular services, dining, and public spaces; administrative staff occupy the third floor. The ambassador's suite, offices for personal staff, and a library/meeting room are located on the top floor. Colors and patterns representing the flora of the "garden city" are applied selectively to fabrics, textures, and wall surfaces.

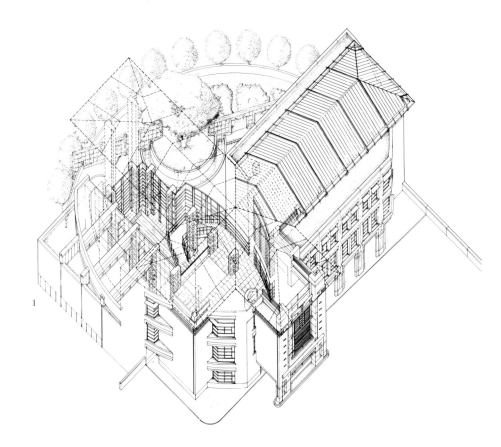

1

2

1 Axonometric
2 Exterior view
3 Main conference room
4 Entry level plan
5 Exterior view of lobby/atrium

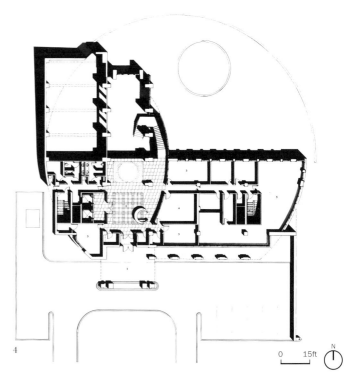

4

0   15ft   N

5

A monumental stair leads from the entry level to the garden courtyard below. A diagonal stone wall separates the upper paved garden terrace, which is used for diplomatic receptions, from the lower, more informal perennial flower garden.

Major exterior materials include brick, limestone and granite trim; clear glass; and a lead-coated metal roof. Mahogany and bubinga are strategically incorporated to enrich the texture and detail of the chancery, reflecting the tropical qualities of Singapore.

6

7

8

9

US Capitol Visitor Center

Design/Completion 1995/2000
Washington, DC
Architect of the Capitol
450,000 square feet
Slurry wall construction with concrete structure
Granite plaza with exterior granite and marble accents

RTKL's design of the US Capitol Visitor Center represents the last major addition in the thoughtful evolution of this historic structure.

Designed to accommodate 2,000 visitors per hour, the facility will be located under the East Plaza to preserve views of the Capitol, respect the original Frederick Law Olmsted landscape plan, and enhance security while maintaining an atmosphere of free public access. The plaza itself will be redesigned to create a pedestrian setting more appropriate to this symbol of America's democratic system.

Approximately half of the visitor center is devoted to public and administrative areas, exhibition space, a gift shop, orientation theaters, and food service facilities. The balance of the space is reserved for a film auditorium for the Library of Congress and future expansion needs.

RTKL's work on the visitor center builds on earlier assignments for the Architect of the Capitol that range from security studies to renovation and new construction in the House and Senate office buildings.

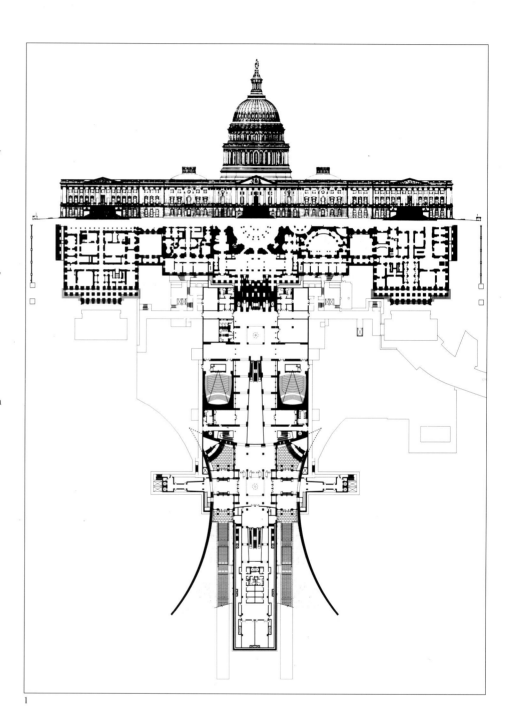

1

1   Section/plan
2   View of the Capitol
3   Reverse section/plan

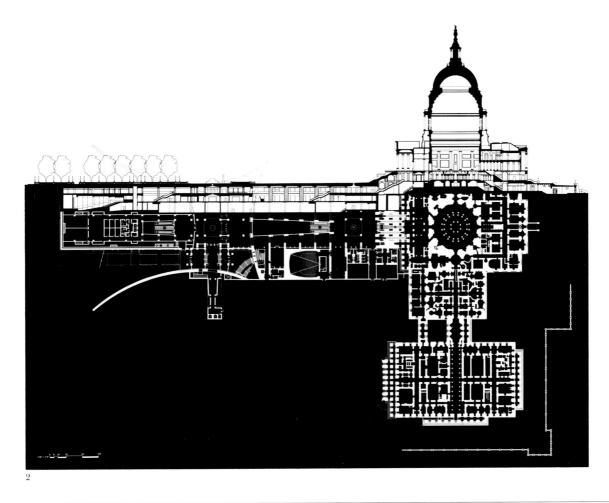

2

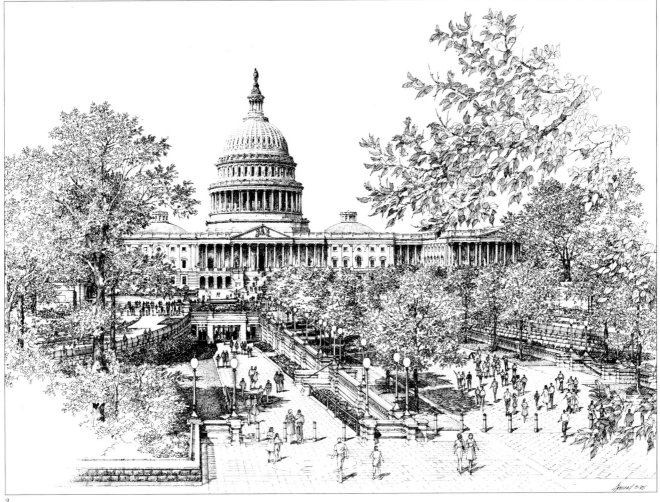

3

RTKL Board of Directors

FIRM PROFILE

Statement of Philosophy

This Statement of Philosophy expresses our firm's basic values and corporate objectives. It is based upon our history, our corporate culture, and the vision of our leaders. It builds upon the four aspects of our work that contribute to our success: design, clients, people, and management. This Statement expresses what we are and what we aspire to become.

Design is the essence of all we do; our professional activities are focused on one single purpose—serving human needs by creating a humane environment. Everyone has a role and a responsibility in achieving projects of the highest design quality. For this reason, we stress the team rather than departments. We strive for design excellence, technical quality, and the highest level of professional service.

RTKL serves and seeks clients equally committed to excellence. We develop ongoing relationships in which we fulfill our clients' demands for a high level of service and high-quality products. Every RTKL employee helps to live this philosophy. The resulting success accrues equally to our clients and our firm.

The quality of our firm and our work depends on the quality of our people. We seek to attract and retain individuals of exceptional talent and enthusiasm who share our commitment to excellence. We encourage and support professional growth within a team environment that encompasses the entire firm as a unified entity. In this way, we support the team in its broadest sense, drawing upon the resources and expertise of everyone at RTKL.

We are first and foremost design professionals; the corporate organization is secondary to the operation of the team and supports the needs of the team in producing its projects. We have successfully sought to maintain a stable corporate entity that continually seeks to improve itself through sound business practices in a competitive, constantly changing world. This allows us to expand technologically and geographically, while putting design, clients, and people first.

RTKL is a demanding place in which to work. We value hard work, honesty, and straight dealing. It is our job to solve complicated problems. Through the collective talents of the highest caliber of people, we produce solutions of enduring value, ranging in scale from city plans to the printed page. Moreover, we recognize the contribution that each of our employees makes in accomplishing these tasks and in promoting the health of our organization.

DESIGN

Our humanistic attitude derives from the firm's roots in urban design. This work internalized values such as commitment to revitalizing cities, making a positive contribution to the environment, searching for the "human scale," shaping outdoor spaces according to their use, and generally designing with and for people.

We strive for compelling design. While we seek innovation, it is not at the expense of time-tested solutions. We value experience. We seek to create projects with a coherent overall composition. We believe that architects, engineers, and specialists in diverse fields should push technology to its limits but always to serve human purposes and our clients' needs. The order in our design is the result of the design team's effort to creatively, realistically, and simply balance the numerous facts and forces affecting the design.

We strive for design excellence, technical quality, and professional service. Our work is characterized by consistent thoroughness and professionalism and of a quality expected of a firm of our experience and resources. Our services communicate our sense of responsibility and shared commitment to each project.

CLIENTS

We are attentive to the needs of our clients. By listening with an open mind and an educated ear, we are able to gain an appreciation of the functional, economic, and cultural circumstances that broadly define each project. With that understanding, we work with our clients to synthesize these challenges and constraints into solutions that are technically and aesthetically appropriate and responsive to the needs of our clients and society.

The manner in which we do our work is important. Every task should be done properly and within the client's time and budget constraints. Working diligently and intelligently increases productivity and delivers to our clients a quality service and product at a reasonable cost.

We thrive on repeat business and strong relationships with our clients. Such relationships are built on mutual respect, courtesy, integrity, helpfulness, and, most of all, by delivering design excellence and quality service. By drawing upon our creative ability, expertise, experience, and enthusiasm, we intend to go beyond our clients' expectations.

PEOPLE

All we are and all we do involves people. From a humanistic commitment to designing distinctive architecture to our care for those with whom we work, people are at the core of our philosophy. We hope to provide a forum in which talented individuals may reach their fullest potential and collectively generate products of lasting value. Our success and our reputation both depend on developing people who are capable, enthusiastic about their work, and proud of their own and their firm's accomplishments.

We believe strongly that each of us can learn from his or her colleagues; the notion of teamwork is critical to our philosophy. Our work and our projects are too complex for the individual professional to accomplish alone. In a team, each person brings to the effort differing perspectives, skills, and degrees of experience, all blending to create a far greater whole. By emphasizing the individual's ability to excel within the team, we can bring out the best in each member.

We encourage each team to share information and staff to promote the firm as a unified entity. In this way, we support the team in its broadest sense, drawing upon the resources and expertise of everyone at RTKL. We seek to provide a challenging atmosphere for professional long-term growth, development, and success. In return, we expect RTKL employees to meet high standards of professional performance, to be flexible, and to be responsive to changing project needs. We value hard work, a positive "can-do" attitude, and enthusiasm. We also believe in a balance between the responsibilities our employees have to the firm and to their personal lives.

We believe in and actively promote affirmative action in hiring and by providing opportunities for advancement. Advancement in the firm is based upon an individual's record of professional achievement, initiative, application of talent, and interpersonal skills. We expect senior professionals to continue to grow as well as nurture and help develop the talents and abilities of less experienced individuals. By promoting from within whenever possible, the long-term growth and development of our staff remains a fundamental element of our success.

MANAGEMENT

Although organized as a corporation for reasons of financial and operational efficiency, the firm functions as a group of studios or teams led by their respective principals. The studio framework gives us a greater degree of organization and coherence while allowing us the freedom and small-team approach we require.

Ownership of the firm is not in the hands of a few. As the firm has grown, the ownership has been shared more broadly and has re-generated. Succession of ownership and leadership is viewed as a long-term, continuing process with professionals encouraged to take on increasing leadership responsibilities.

RTKL's long-standing policy has been to manage our professional activities through sound business practices. We reinvest a substantial share of profits back into the firm. This reinvestment has financed the establishment of our national and international offices, the full implementation of advanced computerization systems, and our professional education programs.

The health of our organization is important to our clients, especially those who are undertaking major projects or are interested in establishing or maintaining long-term or national/international relationships with us. The health of our organization is also important to our people, with regard to professional growth, employee benefits, and continuity of employment.

Ours is a very competitive profession and business. To be profitable in such a marketplace requires our services and our projects to be of the highest caliber, our staff productive and fairly compensated, and our organization well-managed. While profitability cannot be overlooked, our philosophy puts design, clients, and people first. Each day's work must be done creatively, enthusiastically, and effectively so that each person's performance contributes to our success.

Biographies

Harold L. Adams FAIA, RIBA, JIA

Chairman and President

Under the leadership of Mr Adams the firm has developed into an international practice with offices in the United States, London, Tokyo, and Hong Kong, and a reputation for design and management expertise. In addition to his fellowship of the American Institute of Architects, Mr Adams holds a "first-class Kenchikushi" license, awarded by Japan's Ministry of Construction and is active as a trustee and board member for a number of Baltimore and Washington arts, education, and civic organizations. Mr Adams received his Bachelor of Architecture degree from Texas A&M University.

David J. Brotman AIA, CSI

Vice Chairman

As well as being vice chairman of the firm, Mr Brotman is also Director of RTKL's Los Angeles office and a member of the firm's executive committee. Under his direction, the Los Angeles office has developed an expanding portfolio of projects throughout the Pacific Rim and the west coast of the United States. Mr Brotman was also instrumental in establishing the firm's Dallas office in 1979, where he combined his management and design strengths as vice president-in-charge of a number of high-profile projects. Mr Brotman received his Bachelor of Science in Architecture degree from the University of Cincinnati.

David C. Hudson AIA, CSI

Executive Vice President

Mr Hudson is director of the Baltimore and Washington offices. His background includes project direction and management from concept design through construction, including development of contract documents and specifications, and construction contract administration for a broad range of mixed-use projects, hotels, specialized educational facilities, office buildings, retail centers, and parking structures. Mr Hudson joined RTKL in 1977 and joined the board in 1992. He received his Bachelor of Architecture degree from Virginia Tech.

David R. Beard AIA

Senior Vice President

Mr Beard is director of RTKL's health sciences group, based in Baltimore, and is responsible for the project management, design, and planning of health-care and research facilities for public and private clients. He joined RTKL in 1971 and became a senior vice president in 1989. Mr Beard received a Bachelor of Architecture degree from Auburn University and a Master of Architecture degree from the University of California, Berkeley.

Gary A. Bowden FAIA

Senior Vice President

Mr Bowden brings to RTKL's board of directors a strong design orientation honed through nearly three decades of professional practice. Since joining RTKL in 1970, he has served as vice president-in-charge on a number of award-winning international mixed-use, retail, and commercial projects. Mr Bowden was promoted to vice president in 1977 and was elected to the board in 1991. His contributions to retail design earned him fellowship of the American Institute of Architects in 1994. Mr Bowden received a Bachelor of Architecture degree from Howard University and a Master of Architecture in Urban Design degree from Carnegie Mellon University.

Paul G. Hanegraaf AIA

Vice President

As managing director of RTKL's London office, Mr Hanegraaf is responsible for the firm's work throughout Europe and the UK. With 15 years of experience with RTKL, he has developed a particular expertise in the design of complex, urban multi-use developments, hotels, and office towers. This has included work in North and South America, Western Europe, and Eastern Europe. A member of the firm's board of directors, Mr Hanegraaf joined RTKL in 1980 and was promoted to vice president in 1992. He received a Bachelor of Science in Architecture degree from the University of Wisconsin and a Master of Architecture degree from the University of Minnesota.

Lance K. Josal AIA

Vice President

Mr Josal is the director of RTKL's Dallas office and an advisory member of the board of directors. He leads a team of experienced designers and project managers on all phases of design and construction for domestic and international projects. He is particularly knowledgeable in the areas of retail mall renovations and vertical expansions. Mr Josal joined RTKL in 1979, was named associate vice president in 1985, vice president in 1992, and managing director of the Dallas office in 1994. Mr Josal received a Bachelor of Architecture degree and a Bachelor of Arts, Architectural Studies, degree from North Dakota State University, Fargo.

Robert R. Manfredi PE, CEM

Senior Vice President

Mr Manfredi is director of RTKL's mechanical/electrical/ plumbing engineering studio, which has been an instrumental component of RTKL for 20 years. He is a member of the Association of Energy Engineers and has been a Certified Energy Manager since 1982. He has engineering, technical, and administrative experience in virtually every type of project, including high-tech and manufacturing facilities, office, retail, hotels, and health-care. An author and lecturer on intelligent building systems, computer-aided design, and solar energy, Mr Manfredi has been published in professional journals and is an active member of a number of professional societies. He joined RTKL in 1979 and was appointed to the board of directors in 1985. Mr Manfredi was educated at the University of Maryland and George Washington University.

Ted A. Niederman AIA

Senior Vice President/Secretary

Mr Niederman has been a member of the board of directors since 1985 and a vice president since 1970. He has three decades of experience in all phases of project planning, administration, and implementation. As director of one of the firm's architectural design studios, he has headed up diverse major architectural projects for public- and private-sector clients. These include high-technology facilities for corporate clients, educational and institutional facilities, and governmental and military facility programs. Mr Niederman received a Bachelor of Architecture degree from the Massachusetts Institute of Technology.

Board of Directors

Vice Presidents

Sudhakar G. Thakurdesai AIA

Senior Vice President

Mr Thakurdesai's training and expertise in the fields of architecture, planning, and urban design emphasize an interdisciplinary approach to the development of design solutions and strategies for complex physical planning problems. He has an extensive portfolio of projects in the United States as well as major international experience in Australia, North America, and Southeast Asia. Mr Thakurdesai joined RTKL in 1979 and was promoted to vice president in 1987. Mr Thakurdesai received a Certificate of Higher Studies in Ekistics (Community and Regional Planning) from the Athens Center of Ekistics, Greece, and a Master of Architecture degree from the Harvard Graduate School of Design.

Jonathan D. Bailey AIA

Jonathan Bailey, director of RTKL's health sciences group based in Dallas, has been actively involved in health facility planning, programming, and design for a variety of medical and commercial projects, totalling one billion dollars of construction cost. Mr Bailey earned his Master of Architecture degree from Texas A&M University with an emphasis in health facility planning and interior design.

Dianne Blair Black AIA

Ms Black's experience and education have focused on the management of complex corporate and institutional projects. She is experienced in master and strategic planning, programming and space planning, facility analysis, and the use of computer applications through all phases of project development. She joined RTKL in 1979 and was made a vice president of the firm in 1994. Ms Black received a Bachelor of Architecture degree from the University of Minnesota, Minneapolis, and a Master of Administrative Science degree from Johns Hopkins University.

Karen Koenig Blose Esq.

General Counsel

Ms Koenig Blose, RTKL's in-house counsel, joined the firm in 1990 after representing RTKL in various legal matters as outside counsel during the preceding 10 years. She was promoted to vice president in 1993. Ms Koenig Blose received a Bachelor of Arts degree from Mount Holyoke College and a Juris Doctor degree from Duke University School of Law.

Barton R. Chambers AIA

Based in Los Angeles, Mr Chambers has been responsible for a wide range of projects throughout the world, including large-scale multi-use developments and retail centers, particularly those involving complex renovations. Mr Chambers joined RTKL in 1980. He received a Bachelor of Architecture degree from the University of Texas at Austin and attended the University of Oklahoma and the University of Calgary.

Rose M. Dela Vega

Ms Dela Vega serves as RTKL's director of federal contracts and marketing, responsible for identifying, securing, and negotiating the firm's work in the public sector. She joined the firm in 1991 after a distinguished career with the Chesapeake Division, Naval Facilities Engineering Command, bringing with her particular expertise in federal procurement procedures and contracts.

Ann L. Dudrow

Ms Dudrow was responsible for establishing RTKL's Graphics Group and served as its co-director for many years. Now based in Los Angeles, she has developed a diverse portfolio and is considered a recognized leader in the field of environmental graphics. Her work has won numerous awards and accolades. She received a Bachelor of Fine Arts degree from the Rhode Island School of Design.

Phillips S. Engelke

As director of graphics, Mr Engelke is responsible for the design and management of environmental and print graphics programs for major international and national retail, office, hotel, and resort projects. Mr Engelke has served as art director at a number of television stations and also has a strong background in advertising and promotion. He was promoted to vice president in 1990. Mr Engelke received a Bachelor of Fine Arts degree from the Philadelphia College of Art.

Ronald E. Fidler AIA, CSI

Mr Fidler directs the development and implementation of design and contract documents for a variety of project types. His recent experience includes a number of major public sector projects, corporate facilities, and large office buildings. He joined RTKL in 1964 and was made a vice president in 1984. Mr Fidler received a Bachelor of Fine Arts degree from the Maryland Institute, Baltimore.

Norman M. Garden AIA

Mr Garden has served as project manager
and designer on a number of large-scale,
mixed-use projects and regional malls.
He has developed expertise in the design
of integrated, multi-use developments
and the renovation of existing facilities.
Mr Garden joined RTKL in 1982, and
was promoted to vice president in 1993.
He received a Bachelor of Architecture
degree from the University of Minnesota,
Minneapolis.

John R. Gosling ARIBA, AICP

Mr Gosling joined RTKL in 1984 as
director of planning and urban design in
the Dallas office. He has served as senior
planner on a variety of public sector,
corporate, commercial, and new
community projects throughout the
nation. His two decades of planning
experience include downtown
revitalization, site development, project
feasibility analysis, development
programming, land-use planning, and
urban design. Mr Gosling was named a
vice president of the firm in 1988. He
received his degree from the Architectural
Association School of Architecture,
London.

Jeffrey J. Gunning AIA

Mr Gunning is a senior project designer
in RTKL's Dallas office. Since joining
RTKL in 1984 he has developed
international credentials in the design
of complex retail-driven developments,
particularly those combining hotel,
entertainment, and office uses.
Mr Gunning received a Bachelor of
Architecture degree and a Bachelor
of Science degree in Environmental
Design from the University of
Oklahoma, Norman.

D. Rodman Henderer AIA

Mr Henderer has emerged as one of RTKL's most talented designers, experienced in all phases of project development from conception through construction administration. His portfolio of international and domestic assignments encompasses embassies, hotels and resorts, office, retail, mixed-use, and health-care projects. Mr Henderer joined RTKL in 1984 and was promoted to vice president in 1992. He received his Bachelor of Architecture degree from Syracuse University and attended the Architectural Association School of Architecture, London.

Paul F. Jacob III AIA

Mr Jacob is one of the founding vice presidents of RTKL's Los Angeles office. His extensive design portfolio ranges from large-scale urban mixed-use projects to regional retail centers, hotels, and entertainment-based projects. He joined RTKL in 1970 and was promoted to vice president in 1986. Mr Jacob received his Bachelor of Architecture degree from Carnegie Mellon University.

Pablo Laguarda AIA

One of the firm's most talented designers, Mr Laguarda is a senior architect who has nearly two decades of architectural experience and an impressive portfolio of hotel, resort and mixed-use projects. Mr Laguarda joined RTKL in 1988 and was named a vice president in 1995.

Todd C. Lundgren AIA

Mr Lundgren joined RTKL in 1980
and has emerged as a leader in the
firm's hospitality industry work. His
experience on a wide variety of project
types has allowed him to direct RTKL
teams through all phases of design,
production and construction, as well as
managing multiple consultant teams.
Mr Lundgren received a Bachelor of
Architecture degree from the University
of Cincinnati.

Donald A. McConnell CPA

Treasurer

Mr McConnell is RTKL's director of
finance. His varied financial experience
makes him uniquely qualified as a leader
in financial reporting, cash flow
management, and general business issues.
Mr McConnell joined RTKL in 1974 and
was promoted to vice president in 1984.
He received his Bachelor of Science in
Business from Pennsylvania State
University and is a Certified Public
Accountant in the State of Maryland.

Thom McKay

Mr McKay joined the firm in 1985
to manage the marketing and
communications efforts in the
headquarters office. He moved to
London in 1990 and was instrumental
in establishing the office there and
broadening RTKL's European presence.
He returned to Baltimore in 1996 to
direct the firm's strategic services. He
received a Bachelor of Arts degree from
Georgetown University and attended the
University of London.

Candace K. Sheeley AIA, CSI

Ms Sheeley is a senior project director in RTKL's London office, and is responsible for guiding a project from inception through completion. She has developed a particular expertise in complex refurbishments, especially in the retail sector, and has managed some of the firm's most successful retail renovations. Ms Sheeley joined RTKL in 1981 and was made a vice president in 1994. She received a Bachelor of Architecture degree from Kansas State University.

Robert D. Smith AIA, APA

As director of planning and urban design for RTKL's Los Angeles office, Mr Smith has 25 years of experience in a variety of architectural, land development, and urban design projects. His extensive portfolio includes large-scale mixed-use developments, retail and office centers, new communities and housing, hotels and resorts, downtown redevelopment, and town centers. Mr Smith was named a vice president of the firm in 1992. He received his Bachelor of Architecture degree from Case Western Reserve University and a Master of City Planning degree from the University of Michigan.

Stephen Spinazzola PE

Mr Spinazzola has more than a decade of experience in both mechanical design and project management on a wide range of projects. Specializing in HVAC design, he was a member of RTKL's Mechanical and Electrical studio from 1981 to 1991. He re-joined the firm in 1995 as a vice president. Mr Spinazzola received a Bachelor of Architectural Engineering from the Pennsylvania State University.

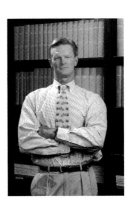

Daun Paul St Amand AIA

Mr St Amand joined RTKL in 1989
bringing 13 years of experience in all
aspects of architecture and construction.
Based in Los Angeles, he has developed
a diverse portfolio but has come to
specialize in the design of residential
and office towers. Mr St Amand received
a Bachelor of Architecture degree from
the University of Southern California
School of Architecture.

David Vere Thompson AIA

Mr Thompson has experience on a wide
range of architectural and facility
planning projects, with an emphasis on
large-scale, advanced technology facilities
masterplanning, design, and project
management. He has also played a major
role in the development and application
of firmwide computer-aided design and
planning systems. Mr Thompson joined
RTKL in 1974 and was named a vice
president in 1993. He received a Bachelor
of Environmental Design degree from
the University of Wisconsin and a Master
of Architecture degree from Texas A&M
University.

Thomas R. Witt AIA

Mr Witt joined RTKL in 1968 and
was named a vice president in the RTKL
Dallas office in 1981. He has served as
either vice president-in-charge or design
principal on a broad range of projects
including retail and mixed-use
developments, office buildings, hotels,
educational facilities, and civic buildings.
He received a Bachelor of Architecture
degree from Pennsylvania State University.

Bernard J. Wulff AIA

Mr Wulff is director of architecture in RTKL's Washington office. Under his leadership the office has developed an impressive international portfolio of office, interior, government, hotel and resort, retail, and mixed-use projects. Mr Wulff joined RTKL in 1964 and was promoted to vice president in 1981. He received his Bachelor of Science degree from the University of Cincinnati and a Master of Architecture degree from the Massachusetts Institute of Technology.

Gregory A. Yager AIA

Mr Yager is the manager of RTKL's Hong Kong office. A talented project architect, Mr Yager offers extensive experience in the design and master-planning of large-scale office, and multi-use facilities. Mr Yager joined RTKL in 1980 and was promoted to vice president in 1994. He received a Bachelor of Architecture degree from Kansas State University and a Master of Architecture degree from the University of Minnesota.

Chronological List of Selected Buildings and Projects

* Indicates work featured in this book
(See Selected and Current Works)

Academic/Education

The Park School[1]
Baltimore, MD
The Park School, 1962

Goucher College[2]
College Center and Kraushaar
Auditorium
Towson, MD
Goucher College, 1964

**Anne Arundel Community College
Resource Center**
Annapolis, MD, 1965

Anne Arundel County Branch Library
Harundale, MD, 1968

South County Public Library
Deale, MD
Town of Deale, 1969

St Johns College
Library Addition
Annapolis, MD, 1969

Anne Arundel Community College[3]
Anne Arundel County, MD
Anne Arundel Community College, 1970

University of Maryland[4]
Baltimore County Campus
Catonsville, MD
University of Maryland System, 1970

**Performing Arts Center
St Timothy's School**[5]
Stevenson, MD
St Timothy's School, 1971

St Mary's Seminary
(Interior Renovation)
Baltimore, MD, 1974

Southwestern High School[6]
Baltimore, MD
Baltimore City Public Schools, 1975

Corning Public Library[7]
Corning, NY
City of Corning, 1976

Dundalk Community College[8]
Performing Arts Center
Baltimore, MD
Dundalk Community College, 1978

Dundalk Community College
Learning Resource Center
Dundalk, MD, 1979

University of Maryland[9]
Baltimore County Campus Library
Catonsville, MD, 1980

USF&G Mount Washington Campus
Baltimore, MD
USF&G, 1984

***The Johns Hopkins Hospital
Redevelopment 1973–1983**
Baltimore, MD
The Johns Hopkins Hospital, 1984

IBM Education Center at Thornwood
Thornwood, NY
IBM Corporation, 1986

Rosemont Performing Arts Center
Rosemont, IL
Melvin Simon & Associates, Inc. and
Hawthorn Realty, 1986

*AT&T Customer Technology Center
Dallas, TX
AT&T Real Estate, 1988

Digital Equipment Corporation
Corporate Education Center
Boylston, MA
Digital Equipment Corporation, 1988

Institute for Islamic and Arabic Studies in America
Islamic Saudi Academy
Fairfax, VA, 1988

Johns Hopkins University[10]
Mind/Brain Institute
Baltimore, MD
Johns Hopkins University, 1988

University Center
Ashburne, VA
The Charles E. Smith Companies
and Michael Swerdlow Companies, 1988

Sumner School
Washington, DC
Boston Properties and the Washington
DC Public School System, 1990

*Sculpture Studio
Baltimore, MD
Maryland Institute, College of Art, 1990

Shrewsbury Public Schools
Prototype Design
Shrewsbury, MA, 1991

University of Maryland
Dental School
Baltimore, MD
University of Maryland at Baltimore, 1991

Georgetown University
Academic Facility
Washington, DC
Georgetown University, 1992

The Johns Hopkins Bayview Research Campus
Baltimore, MD
Dome Corporation/Johns Hopkins
Bayview Medical Center, 1995

University of Virginia
Health Sciences Center
Charlottesville, VA
University of Virginia, 1995

Living Classroom Maritime Institute
Environmental Education Pavilion and
Observation Tower
Baltimore, MD
The Living Classrooms Foundation, 1995

Dundee-Saltpeter Environmental Park[11]
Baltimore, MD
Baltimore County Department of
Parks & Recreation, 1997

United States Naval Academy, Bancroft Hall
Annapolis, MD
Naval Facilities Engineering Command,
Engineering Field Activity Chesapeake
2002

Entertainment/Leisure

Great Adventure World
Jackson, N J
Six Flaggs Corporation, 1981

Queensport
Long Beach, CA
Wrather Corporation, 1987

Disney Island Concept Study
Walt Disney World
Orlando, FL
Walt Disney Imagineering, 1988

Disneyland Resort Hotel Study
Anaheim, CA
The Walt Disney Company, 1988

Arlington Entertainment District
Arlington, TX
Johnson Creek Development
Committee, 1988

Moji Harbor Redevelopment Plan
Kyushu Island, Japan
Seiyo•Corporation, 1989

Star Diamond Center
Taipei, Taiwan
Confidential, 1989

Lyon Retail/Leisure Master Plan
Lyon, France
Longbow PLC, 1990

ET's Adventure
Universal Studios Hollywood
Los Angeles, CA
MCA Recreation Services, 1991

Kishiwada Port Redevelopment
Kishiwada, Japan
Kishiwada Port Development
Corporation, 1991

*Starway Escalator System[1]
Universal Studios Hollywood
Los Angeles, CA
MCA Recreation Services, 1991

Studio Commissary
Universal Studios Hollywood
Los Angeles, CA
MCA Recreation Services, 1991

*Port Orleans and Dixie Landings[2]
Orlando, FL
Disney Development Company, 1992

*Camden Yards Sports Complex[3]
Baltimore, MD
Maryland Stadium Authority and HOK
Sports Facilities Group, 1992

Undersea World
Jakarta, Indonesia
Lippoland Development, 1993

East Asia Theme Park
Confidential, 1993

Jurong Lake Master Plan
Singapore
Technology Parks Pty Ltd, 1993

*Reston Pavilion[4]
Reston, VA
Reston Town Center Associates, 1993

*Shae-Zee Island[5]
Taipei, Taiwan
Taipei Department of City Planning, 1993

**Universal Studios Master Plan
and Site Feasibility Study**
Melun-Senart, France
MCA Recreation Services, 1993

Atlantic City Gateway Project
Atlantic City, NJ
Casino Reinvestment Development
Authority, 1993

Glendale Marketplace
Glendale, CA
JMB/Urban Development Co., 1993

**Aberdeen Marina Club,
Children's Play Area**
Hong Kong
The Aberdeen Marina Club, 1994

Paramount
Manila, Philippines
Paramount Holdings Equities Inc., 1994

Pinklao Entertainment Centre
Bangkok, Thailand
Central Group of Companies, 1994

Rokko Island Gateway[6]
Kobe, Japan
Seiyo•Corporation, 1994

Seacon Square
Bangkok, Thailand
Seacon Development Group, 1994

Lisbon EXPO '98
Lisbon, Portugal
Parque Expo '98, 1995

*MCA Backlot Tram Facility
Universal Studios Hollywood
Los Angeles, CA
MCA/Universal Studios, 1995

Warner Bros. Cinema[7]
Leicester, England
Warner Bros. Cinemas, 1995

Aberdeen Marina Club Ice Rink
Hong Kong
Kerry Properties, 1995

***The Entertainment Center
at Irvine Spectrum**[8]
Irvine, CA
The Irvine Company, 1995

*China Gate
Inchon Song-Do, Korea
Confidential, 1995

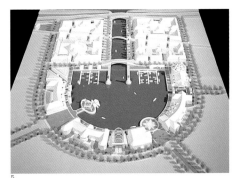

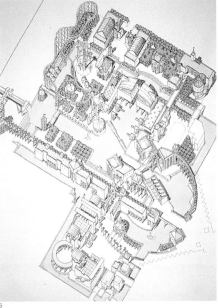

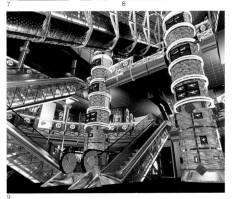

Janss Marketplace
Thousand Oaks, CA
Janss Corporation, 1996

Multiplex Cinemas
Various locations, UK
Warner Bros. Cinemas, 1996

*The Trocadero[9]
London, England
Burford Group plc, 1996

Virgin/MGM Cinema
London, England
Virgin/MGM Cinemas, 1996

Universal City Master Plan
Los Angeles, CA
MCA Recreation Services, 1996

IMAX Cinema
London, England
Burford Group plc, 1996

Centro Park and Promenade[10]
Oberhausen, Germany
Neue Mitte Projektenwicklung GmbH &
Co. KG, a subsidiary of the Stadium Group
1996

Cribbs Causeway Leisure Centre
Bristol, England
Prudential Portfolio Managers, 1998

Fenix Park Leisure Village
Genk, Belgium
Stadium Developments Ltd, 1999

Lotte World
Tokyo, Japan
Lotte World, 2000

Hospitality

Hyatt Regency Baltimore[1]
Baltimore, MD
The Hyatt Corporation, 1974

Smith Bay Vista
St Thomas, Virgin Islands
The Hilmon Company, 1981

St Lucia Conrad Hilton International
St Lucia, West Indies
RMS Associates, 1981

The Palmas Inn[2]
Palmas del Mar, Puerto Rico
Sea Pines Plantation Company, 1981

Princess Hotel[3]
Hamilton, Bermuda
Princess Hotels International, 1983

EcuMed Conference Center
Ft Lauderdale, FL
Tishman Speyer Properties, 1983

Westin Canal Place
New Orleans, LA
Joseph C. Canizaro Interests, 1984

Hyatt Regency Cincinnati
Cincinnati, OH
Prudential Insurance Company and
The Hyatt Corporation, 1984

Radisson Hotel
Burlington, VT
The Kevin F. Donohoe Company, 1985

*Hyatt Regency Grand Cayman
Grand Cayman Island,
British West Indies
Ellesmere (Cayman) Ltd, 1986

Radisson Suites Hotel
Indianapolis, IN
Duke Associates and
Prudential Insurance Company, 1986

Marriott's Orlando World Center[4]
Orlando, FL
Marriott Corporation, 1986

*Grand Hyatt Washington
Washington, DC
Quadrangle Development Corporation
1987

Augusta Hotel
Augusta, GA
The Belz Company, 1987

Marriott Forrestal Village Hotel[5]
Princeton, NJ
Toombs Development Company, 1987

InterContinental Hotels
Building Evaluations
London, England
Edinburgh, Scotland
Paris, France
Cannes, France
Brussels, Belgium
Vienna, Austria
Cologne, Germany
Dusseldorf, Germany
Munich, Germany
Wiesbaden, Germany
Luxembourg
Rome, Italy
Madrid, Spain
Cairo, Egypt
Nairobi, Kenya
Kinshasa, Zaire
Sydney, Australia
Rio de Janeiro, Brazil
Cancun, Mexico
The Seiyo•Corporation, 1988

The Willoughby Bay Resort and Club
Antigua
The Sunshine Corporation, 1988

Izu Peninsula
Nishina, Japan
Alpha Resorts, 1988

*The Bellevue[6]
Philadelphia, PA
Richard I. Rubin & Co., Inc., 1988

Hotel Siam
Bangkok, Thailand
InterContinental Hotels, 1989

Moji Harbor Redevelopment Plan
Kyushu, Japan
The Seiyo•Corporation, 1989

Hyatt Charlotte[7]
Charlotte, NC
Hyatt Development Corporation, 1989

San Antonio Marriott Rivercenter[8]
San Antonio, TX
Marriott Corporation, 1989

Griffin Conference Center
Windsor, CT
Culbro Industries, 1989

Sogo Pernas Center
Kuala Lumpur, Malaysia
Taisei Corporation, 1990

Karuizawa Golf Course Clubhouse/Hotel
Nagano Prefecture, Japan
Dai Nippon Construction, 1990

Chiburi Lake Golf Resort
Tochigi Prefecture, Japan
Kajima Corporation and
Japan View Hotel Co., Ltd, 1990

Golf Resort
Mallorca, Spain
Kajima Corporation, 1990

Hotel des Indes
The Hague, Netherlands
InterContinental Hotels, 1990

*St Andrews Old Course Hotel[9]
St Andrews, Scotland
Old Course Limited and
The Zimmer Group, 1990

Marriott Suites Bethesda
Bethesda, MD
The Charles E. Smith Companies,
The Artery Organization Inc.,
The Floyd E. Davis Jr Family,
The Charles A. Camalier Jr Family,
Marriott Corporation, 1990

The Ritz-Carlton Cleveland[10]
Cleveland, OH
Tower City Hotel Associates, 1990

Hyatt Regency Reston[11]
Reston, VA
Reston Town Center Associates, 1990

Forsgate Conference Center
Monroe Township, NJ
R.H. Development Company, 1990

Hotel Britannia
London, England
InterContinental Hotels, 1991

*The Manhattan(12)
Makuhari, Chiba Prefecture, Japan
Kajima Corporation; NESCO Co. Ltd,
1991

Japanese Resort
Shizuoka Prefecture, Japan
Withheld, 1991

*Hotel Amstel(13)
Amsterdam, The Netherlands
InterContinental Hotels, 1992

May Kiss Restaurant(14)
Tokyo, Japan
Seiyo•Continental Hotels Ltd, 1992

Niseko West Valley Resort Community
Iwani Beach, Japan
Tsukamoto Sangyo Co. Ltd, 1992

Iguatemi Hotel
São Paulo, Brazil
La Fonte Empressa de Shopping
Centers, 1992

The Ritz-Carlton Hotel
White Plains, NY
Mall Properties and Ritz-Carlton, 1992

Regalleon Plaza
Philadelphia, PA
Asbell and Associates, 1992

Marriott at Pelican Hill
Irvine, CA
Marriott Corporation, 1992

***Port Orleans
and Dixie Landings**
Orlando, FL
Disney Development Company, 1992

Takeshiba Hotel
Tokyo, Japan
Seiyo•Continental Hotels Ltd, 1993

Rokko Island Hotel
Kobe, Japan
Seiyo•Corporation, 1993

**Hyatt Regency Canmore at
Banff National Park**(15)
Canmore, Alberta, Canada
Canmore Alpine Development
Company Ltd, 1993

Seafer Center InterContinental
Surabaya, Indonesia
PT Seafer Hotel International, 1993

Ciawi Country Club
Ciawi/Bogor, Indonesia
PT Pamada Jaya, 1993

Senayan Square (Hotel)
Jakarta, Indonesia
Kajima Overseas Asia, a subsidiary of
Kajima Corporation, 1994

Oak Valley Resort
Kang-Wan Do, Korea
The International Resort Corporation
1994

Merlin Sheraton Hotels
Penang, Malaysia
Merlin Management Corporation, 1994

Malaysian International Destination Resort
Johor Baharu, Malaysia
Confidential

Resort Hotel at Sea Village
Chejudo Island, Korea
Marriott International, 1994

Sheraton Hotel
South Padre Island, TX
Swan Court Hotels, 1994

***Harborside Hyatt Conference
Center and Hotel**(16)
Boston, MA
Logan Harborside Associates II Limited
Partnership, 1995

Batulao Resort
Luzon, Philippines
Landco, 1995

Canyonwoods Hotel
Luzon, Philippines
Landco, 1995

11

12

13

14

Bona City Hotel
Cilegon, Indonesia
Bonauli Real Estate, 1995

Bona Terra Resort
West Java, Indonesia
Bonauli Real Estate, 1995

North Obhur Resort
Jeddah, Saudi Arabia
Saudi Binladin Group, 1995

*Wyndham Hotel at Playhouse Square[17]
Cleveland, OH
Wyndham Hotels and Resorts and
Playhouse Square Foundation, 1995

Shin-Cheju Resort Hotel
Cheju Island, South Korea
Dongwha Investment and Development
Co., Ltd, 1995

Dong-Hae Resort
Kyongju, Korea
Confidential, 1995

*Club Industrial de Monterrey[18]
Monterrey, N.L., Mexico
Club Industrial de Monterrey, 1995

**Westin Hotel and International
Business Center**
Campinas, São Paulo, Brazil
Lix de Cunha Group and
Westin South America, 1996

Disney's Boardwalk Resort
Orlando, FL
Disney Development Company, 1996

Disney's Coronado Springs Resort
Orlando, FL
Disney Development Company, 1996

North Beach
Penang, Malaysia
C.A. Goh Associates, 1997

Amman Sheraton
Amman, Jordan
Al-Dawliyah, 1997

Bali Pecatu Resort
Bali, Indonesia
Putrisekar Maharani, 1998

Omni Bangkok
Bangkok, Thailand
Maneeya Realty Company Ltd, 1998

*Tanjung Aru Master Plan[19]
Kota Kinabalu, Sabah, East Malaysia
Golden Plus Holding Berhad, 1998

Four Seasons Hotel
Riyadh, Saudi Arabia
Kingdom Trade Establishment, 1999

Second Lotte World
Seoul, Korea
Lotte World, 2000

Brazilian Resort
Bahia, Brazil
Odebrecht, S.A.
2005 (phased over 10 years)

Health Sciences

*Greater Baltimore Medical Center
Baltimore, MD, 1966/1993

**New Generation of Military
Hospitals Prototype**
Travis Air Force Base, CA, 1973

**The Johns Hopkins Hospital
Redevelopment**[1]
Baltimore, MD, 1973–84

Sinai Hospital Expansion
Baltimore, MD, 1977

**The National Institutes of
Health Building 13**
Bethesda, MD, 1977

The National Naval Medical Center
Development Plan
Bethesda, MD
Naval Facilities Engineering Command,
Engineering Field Activity Chesapeake,
1978

15

16

17

18

19

1

St Elizabeth Medical Center South[2]
Covington, KY, 1978

Howard County General Hospital
Columbia, MD, 1980

The Memorial Hospital
Easton, MD, 1983

Mount Washington Pediatric Hospital
Baltimore, MD, 1983

**University of Maryland Medical
System Hospital**
Baltimore, MD, 1983–88

Franklin Square Medical Office Building
Baltimore, MD, 1984

Baltimore Biomedical Research Center
Baltimore, MD, 1984

Brooke Army Medical Center
San Antonio, TX
US Army Corps of Engineers,
Fort Worth District, 1985

The Johns Hopkins Hospital
Houck Building
Baltimore, MD, 1985

Walter Reed Army Medical Center
Washington, DC, 1985

Johns Hopkins Bayview Medical Center
Neonatal ICU
Baltimore, MD, 1985

Church Hospital
Baltimore, MD, 1985–87

Tindeco Wharf HMO Clinic
Baltimore, MD, 1986

Anne Arundel General Hospital
Master Plan
Annapolis, MD, 1986

Bowman Grey School of Medicine
Winston-Salem, NC, 1986

**University of Maryland Medical
System Hospital**
Baltimore, MD, 1986

Clinton Farms Retirement Community
Site Master Plan
Clinton, MD, 1986

Maryland General Hospital
Baltimore, MD, 1986

Oliver Plaza HMO Clinic
Baltimore, MD, 1986

Johns Hopkins Bayview Medical Center
Long-Term Care Center
Baltimore, MD, 1986

East Baltimore Medical Center
Baltimore, MD, 1986

Hartford Hospital
Medical Office Building
Hartford, CT, 1986

Johns Hopkins Bayview Medical Center[3]
Master Plan
Dome Corporation/Johns Hopkins
Bayview Medical Center
Baltimore, MD, 1986–88

**University of Maryland Medical Center
Parking Garage**
Baltimore, MD, 1987

Johns Hopkins Hospital
1830 East Monument Street
Baltimore, MD, 1987

Johns Hopkins Bayview Medical Center
Labor/Delivery Suite Renovation
Baltimore, MD, 1987

St Joseph Medical Center
Site Facilities Master Plan
Towson, MD, 1987

Hartford Hospital
Bliss Inpatient Building
Hartford, CT, 1987

Hartford Hospital
Oncology Center
Hartford, CT, 1987

Sinai Hospital
Renovation/Replacement Program
Baltimore, MD, 1987

**Greater Southeast Community Hospital
Campus Plan**
Washington, DC, 1987

University of Maryland
School of Medicine and
Pharmacy/Health Sciences Library
1987–88

Johns Hopkins Bayview Medical Center
Parking Structure
Baltimore, MD, 1988

Johns Hopkins Bayview Medical Center
Central Utilities Plant
Baltimore, MD, 1988

Church Hospital
Nuclear Medicine/EMS/Respiratory
Therapy
Baltimore, MD, 1988

Wyman Park Medical Center
Facility Renovations
Baltimore, MD, 1988

University of Maryland Medical System
Cardiac Catheterization Lab
Baltimore, MD, 1988

University of Maryland Dental School
Baltimore, MD, 1988

National Institutes of Health
Child Life and Neurosciences Research
Facility
Bethesda, MD, 1988

Johns Hopkins Bayview Medical Center
Psychiatric Facility
Baltimore, MD, 1988

Johns Hopkins University
Mind/Brain Institute
Baltimore, MD, 1988

Hartford Hospital
Day Surgery Suite
Hartford, CT, 1988

Greater Baltimore Medical Center
Physicians Pavilion
Owings Mills, MD, 1988

Hartford Hospital
High Building Inpatient Tower
Hartford, CT, 1988–89

Anne Arundel Medical Center
Ambulatory Surgery and Oncology
Treatment Center
Annapolis, MD, 1989

Department of Veterans Affairs
Facility Development Plans
Hampton, VA; Asheville, NC; Lebanon,
PA; Salisbury, NC; Fort Howard, MD;
Lyons, NJ, 1989–94

Union Memorial Hospital
Site and Facilities Master Plan
Baltimore, MD, 1990

**Department of Veterans Affairs
Medical Center**
Clinical Addition and Medical Center
Modernization
Fort Howard, MD, 1990

**University of Maryland Medical System
Master Facility Plan**
Baltimore, MD, 1990

Albert Einstein Medical Center
Master Facility Plan
Philadelphia, PA, 1991

**University of Virginia Health
Sciences Center**
Master Plan
Charlottesville, VA, 1991

Doylestown Hospital[4]
Ambulatory Care Center and Hospital
Expansion
Doylestown, PA, 1992

Newington Children's Hospital
Hartford, CT, 1993

7

8

9

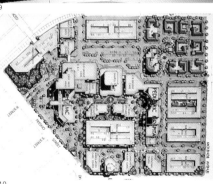

10

Doctors Community Hospital
Ambulatory Services Expansion
Lanham, MD, 1993

DePaul Medical Center
Ambulatory Care Center Addition and
Critical Care Unit Renovations
Norfolk, VA, 1993

**Department of Veterans Affairs
Medical Center**[5]
New Hospital and Outpatient Center
Baltimore, MD, 1993

*Greater Baltimore Medical Center[6,7,8]
Obstetrics/Acute Care Expansion
and Renovation, Baltimore, MD, 1993

Union Memorial Hospital
Cardiovascular Surgery Unit
Baltimore, MD, 1994

Union Memorial Hospital
National Center for Treatment of the
Hand and Upper Extremity
Baltimore, MD, 1994

*Johns Hopkins Bayview Medical Center[9]
Francis Scott Key Pavilion
Baltimore, MD, 1994

**Central California Regional
Medical Center**[10]
Fresno, CA
Community Hospitals of Central
California, 1994

Wayne State University
School of Pharmacy and Allied Health
Academic and Laboratory Program
Detroit, MI, 1994

University of Maryland Medical System
Kernan Hospital Campus Master Plan
Baltimore, MD, 1994

Mercy Medical Center
Center for Women's Health and
Medicine
Baltimore, MD, 1994

Hanover General Hospital
Site and Facilities Master Plan
Hanover, PA, 1995

Georgetown University Medical Center
Outpatient Care Renovations
Pasquerilla Health Care Center
Washington, DC, 1995

Crozer-Chester Medical Center[11]
Pediatric Wing
Upland, PA, 1995

**University of Virginia
Health Sciences Center**
Multistory Building—Adaptive Reuse
Charlottesville, VA, 1995

**University of Virginia Health
Sciences Center**[12]
Jordan Hall Addition
Charlottesville, VA, 1995

Anne Arundel Medical Center[13]
Medical Office Building
Annapolis, MD, 1995

*Anne Arundel Medical Center
Rebecca M. Clatanoff
Women's Hospital
Annapolis, MD, 1995

Detroit Medical Center
Master Facility Plan
Detroit, MI, 1995

Huron Valley Hospital
Master Facility Plan
Commerce Township, MI, 1995

Huron Valley Hospital
Obstetrics and Surgery Addition
Commerce Township, MI, 1995

Grace Hospital
Master Facility Plan
Detroit, MI, 1995

Grace Hospital
Surgery Addition and Lab Renovation
Detroit, MI, 1995

11

12

13

14

Department of Veterans Affairs Medical Center

Outpatient Clinic Addition
Wilmington, DE, 1996

University of Maryland Medical System[14]

William Donald Schaefer Rehabilitation Center at Kernan
Baltimore, MD, 1996

*Summerlin Medical Center

Las Vegas, NV
Universal Health Sciences Inc., 1996

Parkland Memorial Hospital

Dietary Center
Dallas, TX, 1997

The Johns Hopkins Bayview Medical Center

Ambulatory Care Center
Baltimore, MD, 1997

Al Salama Hospital

Saudi Industry and Development Company
Jeddah, Saudi Arabia, 1997

Central California Regional Medical Center

Fresno, CA, TBA

Interior Architecture (1986–present)

International Monetary Fund

Washington, DC
International Monetary Fund, 1986

World Bank

Washington, DC
The World Bank, 1986

*The Center Club

Baltimore, MD
The Center Club, 1986

Bank of Baltimore, Flagship Branch[1]

Baltimore, MD
Bank of Baltimore, 1987

The Riggs National Bank Branch Banks[2]

Washington, DC
Riggs Bank, 1988

Porter/Novelli

Washington, DC
Porter/Novelli, 1988

*AT&T Customer Technology Center

Dallas, Texas
AT&T Real Estate, 1988

Delaware Trust Building[3]

Wilmington, DE
Robinson-Humphrey Properties and Maritime Realty Corp., 1988

Semmes, Bowen & Semmes

Baltimore, MD, 1988

1140 Connecticut Avenue

Washington, DC
The Charles E. Smith Companies, 1989

Catholic Relief Services[4]

Baltimore, MD
Catholic Relief Services, 1989

Alex. Brown & Sons

Baltimore, MD, 1989

2100 Pennsylvania Avenue

Washington, DC
The George Washington University, 1989

Airline Clubs

Los Angeles International, Chicago O'Hare International, New York LaGuardia, West Palm Beach International, and Luis Muñoz Marin International airports.
Continental Airlines, 1989

Team Bank

Bedford, TX
Team Bank, 1990

Bank of Baltimore Headquarters

Baltimore, MD
Bank of Baltimore, 1990

The Baltimore Area Visitors Center

Baltimore, MD
Baltimore Area Convention and Visitors Association, 1990

The Whiting-Turner Contracting Company

Bethesda, MD, 1990

*W.R. Grace & Co.
Boca Raton, FL
W.R. Grace & Co. (interiors), Crocker
& Company (architecture), 1991

Bank One, Texas
Dallas, TX
Bank One, Texas, 1991

*Bank One Cleveland Offices
Cleveland, OH
Banc One Corporation, 1991

T. Rowe Price Operations Center[5]
Owings Mills, MD
T. Rowe Price Associates Inc., 1991

Tydings & Rosenberg[6]
Baltimore, MD, 1991

The Acacia Group
Washington, DC, 1991

Paralyzed Veterans of America
Washington, DC, 1992

Jones, Day, Reavis & Pogue
Tokyo, Japan, 1992

Private Residence at Market Square
Washington, DC
Confidential, 1992

Brown & Wood
Tokyo, Japan, 1992

IBM Requirements and Decisions Lab
Irving, Texas
IBM Corporation, 1992

The Ryland Group Headquarters[7]
Columbia, MD, 1992

*Legg Mason Wood Walker, Inc.
Philadelphia, PA, and other locations
1993

*Dykema Gossett
Washington, DC, 1993

Georgetown University Medical Center
Medical Billing Offices
Washington, DC, 1993

Goodell, DeVries, Leech & Gray
Baltimore, MD, 1993

A. Foster Higgins and Co., Inc.
Washington, DC, 1993

Sterne, Kessler, Goldstein & Fox[8]
Washington, DC, 1993

1225 Connecticut Avenue
Washington, DC
Heitman Properties Ltd, 1994

1250 Connecticut Avenue
Washington, DC
Heitman Properties Ltd, 1994

*Peabody & Brown[9]
Washington, DC, 1994

Semmes, Bowen & Semmes
Washington, DC, 1994

*Coopers & Lybrand[10]
Tysons Corner, VA, 1994

*Embassy of Sweden
Washington, DC
The Government of Sweden, 1995

NFL Players Inc.
Washington, DC
National Football League
Players Association, 1995

The European Union Delegation of the European Commission
Washington, DC, 1995

American Red Cross Headquarters
Washington, DC, 1995

6   7

8

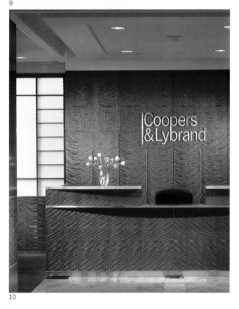

9

10

Multi-use (1980–present)

Center Square
Springfield, MA
Center Square Inc., 1982

Canal Place[1]
New Orleans, LA
Joseph C. Canizaro Interests, 1983

Charleston Town Center
Charleston, WV
Forest City Enterprises, 1983

Lit Block
Philadelphia, PA
Richard I. Rubin & Company, Inc., 1984

189 Peachtree Street
Atlanta, GA
JMB/Federated Realty Associates, Ltd
1984

St Louis Centre[2]
St Louis, MO
Melvin Simon & Associates, Inc., 1985

The Village at Shirlington
Arlington, VA
The Oliver T. Carr Company, 1986

Berkshire Court at Preston Center
Dallas, TX
Kenneth H. Hughes Interests, 1986

Burlington Square
Burlington, VT
American Metropolitan
Development Co., 1986

Central Park at Mid-Cities
Bedford, TX
Wynne/Jackson Inc. and
Kenneth H. Hughes Interests, 1986

Quadrangle[3]
Dallas, TX
The Quadrangle Joint Venture, 1986

Gulf Coast Center
Tampa, FL
JMB Realty Corp. and
JMB/Federated Realty Associates, Ltd
and Collier Enterprises, 1986

Eton Square
Tulsa, OK
Eton Square Associates, 1986

Queensport
Long Beach, CA
Wrather Corporation, 1987

Palmer Square
Princeton, NJ
Collins Development Corporation, 1987

Poplar Shady Grove
East Memphis, TN
The Murphree Company, 1987

Esperanté[4]
West Palm Beach, FL
Esperanté Partnership Ltd, a joint
venture of the John W. Galbreath Co.
and the Hanna-Kent Company, 1988

Fashion Mall at Plantation[5]
Plantation, FL
Melvin Simon & Associates, Inc. and
Deutsch Ireland Properties, 1988

*Pentagon City
Arlington, VA
Melvin Simon & Associates, Inc. and
Rose Associates, Inc., 1988

Park LaBrea
Los Angeles, CA
May Center Inc., 1989

Westlake Center[6]
Seattle, WA
The Rouse Company and
Koehler McFadyen & Company, 1989

Park Central
Phoenix, AZ
The Lehndorff Group, 1989

*Washington Center
Washington, DC
Quadrangle Development Company
1989

*Tower City Center[7]
Cleveland, OH
Forest City Enterprises, 1990

Piney Orchard Village Center
Odenton, MD
The Murphree Company, 1990

*Reston Town Center
Reston, VA
Reston Town Center Associates, 1990

Sogo Pernas Centre
Kuala Lumpur, Malaysia
Taisei Corporation, 1990

Far East Trade Center
Washington, DC
The Alex Conroy Company and
Melvin Simon & Associates, Inc., 1990

Democracy Plaza
Bethesda, MD
The Charles E. Smith Companies,
The Artery Organization, Inc., Davis/
Camalier Families, 1991

Towson Commons[8]
Towson, MD
La Salle Partners Development Limited
1991

Peabody Place
Memphis, TN
Belz Enterprises and the city of
Memphis, 1991

Officers Club Study
Taipei, Taiwan
Sing/Tran Development, 1992

Providence Place at Capital Center
Providence, RI
The Conroy Company; Melvin Simon &
Associates, Inc. and Landow & Co., 1992

Pine Square/Pacific Courts[9]
Long Beach, CA
Janss Corporation, 1992

West Surabaya Town Center
West Surabaya, Indonesia
PT Ciputra Development, 1992

Wadona Shopping Center
Kashiwamura, Japan
Aeon Kosan, 1992

Pittsburgh City Center[10]
Pittsburgh, PA
Pittsburgh City Center Joint Venture
1993

Star Diamond Center
Taipei, Taiwan
Sing/Tran Investment Company, 1993

Central City Bangna
Bangkok, Thailand
Central Department Stores, 1994

Seacon Square
Bangkok, Thailand
Seacon Development Group, 1994

Pinklao
Bangkok, Thailand
Central Pattana Development Co. Ltd
1994

Roxy Plaza
Jakarta, Indonesia
Sinar Mas Group, 1994

Shimoda Center
Akita Prefecture, Japan
Aeon Kosan, 1994

Suluh Fashion Center
Jakarta, Indonesia
PT Risjad Transindo Nasional, 1994

Futtsu Retail Center
Chiba Prefecture, Japan
Aeon Kosan, 1994

Goshono Town Center
Akita, Japan
Aeon Kosan, 1994

Rokko Island Gateway
Kobe, Japan
Seiyo•Corporation, 1994

Hayashibara
Okayama, Japan
Hayashibara/JN Planning, 1994

Hineno Town Center
Hineno, Izumisano, Japan
JUSCO Company Ltd and JMB/Urban
Development Co., 1994

Senayan Square
Jakarta, Indonesia
Kajima Overseas Asia, a subsidiary of
Kajima Corporation, 1994

Yau Yat Tsuen Concept Study
Kowloon Tong, Hong Kong
Swire Properties, 1994

*City Plaza
Taegu, Korea
Confidential, 1995

Omni Marco Polo Hotel Mixed Use Center
Wuhan, China
Golden Resources Ltd, 1995

Pattaya Festival Center[11]
Pattaya, Thailand
Central Group of Companies
1995

Sungai Besi Airbase Site Master Plan
Kuala Lumpur, Malaysia
Metacorp, Berhad, 1995

Citraland Golden Triangle[12]
Jakarta, Indonesia
PT Ciputra Development, 1995

Beijing Ocean Shipping Building
Beijing, China
China Overseas Shipping Company
(COSCO), 1995

Kweillin Plaza
Taipei, Taiwan
LiFu Group, 1996

Grogol Expansion of Citraland
Grogol, Jakarta, Indonesia
PT Ciputra Development, 1996

Daeha Business Centre[13]
Hanoi, Vietnam
Daewoo Corporation, 1996

Raffles City
Singapore
Raffles City Pte. Ltd/DBS Land, Inc.
1996

*Sun DongAn Plaza
Beijing, China
The DongAn Group and Sun Hung Kai
Properties Ltd, a joint venture, 1997

Tsim Sha Tsui Center
Kowloon, Hong Kong
Sino Land Company Ltd, 1997

Colombo[15]
Lisbon, Portugal
SOPASA, 1997

*Rama III
Bangkok, Thailand
Estate Development Company Ltd and
Central Department Stores, 1998

*Urbano Alameda[14]
Mexico City, Mexico
Grupo Arlette, 1998

El Espino
Central America
Inversiones Roble, 1998

*Shanghai Business Center
Shanghai, China
Confidential, 1998

Aeronautical-Science-Technology Tower
Shenzen, China
Shenzen Bian Cheng Enterprise and
Kuang Yu Industrial Holdings Ltd, 1999

***Beijing Bao Xin International
Financial Centre**
Beijing, China
China National Insurance Trust &
Investment Co., 1999

CPPCC Tower
Shenzen, China
Shirble Holdings Ltd, 1999

*Sui Bao Tower
Shenzen, China
Shirble Holdings Ltd, 1998

Guan Hua Plaza
Beijing, China
Beijing Huayuan Real Estate
Corporation, 1999

11

12

13

Chongqing Times Square
Chongqing, China
Wharf (Holdings) Ltd, 1999

Tianjin Mixed Use Project
Tianjin, China
Tianjin Sanloon Enterprise
Development Co., 1999

Beijing Evergreen
Beijing, China
Metro Holdings Limited, 1999

Beijing Times Square
Beijing, China
Wharf (Holdings) Ltd, 1999

American Place
Shanghai, China
KDG Kennard Design Group, 1999

Shiang Shieh Tower
Hangzhou, China
Hangzhou Shiang Shieh Real Estate
Development Co. Ltd, 1999

Perpetual Rose Garden
Hangzhou, China
Foreland Inc., 1999

Xi Xi (Parcel 11)
Beijing, China
Beijing Huayuan Real Estate
Corporation, 1999

Leela Kempinski Mixed Use Center
Bombay, India
Confidential, 1999

Taliraya Mixed Use Center
Jakarta, Indonesia
PT Multifortuna Asindo, 1999

Grand Kuningan
Jakarta, Indonesia
Abadi Guna Papan, 1999

Shanghai Financial Center Plaza[16]
Shanghai, China
China Guotai Securities, 1999

Seafer Centre
Surabaya, Indonesia
PT Seafer General Foods, 1999

Samsung Mixed Use
Taegu, Korea
InfraDesign Inc., 1999

Su Youngbay Landings
Pusan, Korea
Daewoo Corporation, 1999

Daewoo Center[17]
Seoul, Korea
Daewoo Corporation, 1999

North Beach
Penang, Malaysia
C.A. Goh and Associates, 1999

Komtar Mixed Use Project
Penang, Malaysia
Penas Holdings Sdn. Bhd., 1999

Paramount Plaza
Manila, Philippines
Paramount Holdings Equities Inc., 1999

Daya Road Mixed Use
Taichung, Taiwan
Long Ban Construction Co., 1999

Maneeya
Bangkok, Thailand
Maneeya Realty Company Ltd, 1999

Office Buildings

John Deere Regional Office[1]
Timonium, MD
John Deere Equipment Company, 1967

Travelers Insurance Office Building[2]
Hartford, CT
Travelers Insurance Company, 1971

IBM Manassas Virginia Complex
Manassas, VA
IBM Corporation, 1971–1991

14

15

16

17

580 Building
Cincinnati, OH
Western & Southern Life Insurance
1972

Clark Office Building
Columbia, MD
The Rouse Company, 1973

*Charles Center South[3]
Baltimore, MD
Charles Center South Associates, 1975

Environmental Elements Building
Baltimore, MD
Koppers Company Inc., 1975

C&P Office Building
Baltimore, MD
C&P Telephone Company of MD, 1977

*Federated Building[4]
Cincinnati, OH
Federated Department Stores, Inc., 1977

Arvida Financial Plaza
Boca Raton, FL
Arvida Investment Company, 1979

Center Square
Springfield, MA
Center Square, Inc., 1982

Inner Harbor Center
Baltimore, MD
Peter D. Leibowits Company, Inc., 1982

Seven Burlington Square
Burlington, VT
Fidelity Mutual Life Insurance Co.,
American Metropolitan Development
Co., The Kevin F. Donohoe Co., 1983

**Southern Services Office Building
at Perimeter Center**
Atlanta, GA
Taylor & Mathis, 1984

USF+G Mount Washington Campus[5]
Baltimore, MD
USF+G Corporation, 1984, 1991

Berkshire Court at Preston Center
Dallas, TX
Kenneth H. Hughes Interests, 1985

Signet Tower[6]
Baltimore, MD
Signet Bank and the Trammel Crow
Company, 1985

2700 South Quincy Street
Arlington, VA
The Oliver T. Carr Company, 1986

IBM Education Center at Thornwood[7]
Thornwood, NY
IBM Corporation, 1986

Central Park
Bedford, TX
Wynne/Jackson, 1986

One City Centre
St Louis, MO
Cabot, Cabot, & Forbes, 1986

Court Square Building
Baltimore, MD
Kenilworth Equities, Inc., 1986

Computer Sciences Corporation[8]
Phase I—Virginia Technology Center
Falls Church, VA
Computer Sciences Corporation and
Cadillac Fairview Urban Development
Inc., 1986

Quadrangle[9]
Dallas, TX
Kenneth H. Hughes Interests, 1986

Hartford Hospital Medical Office Building
Hartford, CT
Hartford Hospital, 1986

Philadelphia National Bank
Philadelphia, PA
Philadelphia National Bank, 1987

Allentown Road Office Building
Prince George's County, MD
KMS Group, 1987

Redwood Tower[10]
Baltimore, MD
Toombs Development Co., 1987

Democracy Plaza[11,12]
Bethesda, MD
The Charles E. Smith Companies, The
Artery Organization, and
Camalier/Davis Families, 1987

**Kelly-Springfield Tire Company
Corporate Headquarters**
Cumberland, MD
Maryland Economic Development
Corp., 1987

C&P Fairland Data Center
Silver Spring, MD
The C&P Telephone Company of MD
1988

Digital Equipment Corporation
Corporate Education Center
Boylston, MA
Digital Equipment Corporation, 1988

Siemens Office Building
Boca Raton, FL
Siemens Communications Systems, 1988

Computer Sciences Corporation
Phase II—Virginia Technology Center
Falls Church, VA
Cadillac Fairview Urban Development
Inc. and Computer Sciences
Corporation, 1988

Columbia Park, Building 1
Columbia, MD
McGill Development Co., 1988

Plantation Office Building
Plantation, FL
Melvin Simon & Associates, Inc. and
Deutsch Ireland Properties, 1988

Two Hyatt Plaza
Fairfax, VA
The Hazel/Peterson Companies, 1988

Centrepark
West Palm Beach, FL
John W. Galbreath & The Hanna-Kent
Co., and Wolfe Enterprises, Inc., 1988

*The Marsh & McLennan Building[13]
Baltimore, MD
Stone & Associates, Inc., 1989

Columbia Park, Building II
Columbia, MD
McGill Development Co., 1989

One Park Central
Phoenix, AZ
John W. Galbreath & Co. and Lehndorff
Management (USA) Ltd Inc., 1989

Westlake Center Office Building
Seattle, WA
Westlake Center Associates Limited
Partnership, 1989

Washington Center/McLachlen Building
Washington DC
Quadrangle Development Corporation
1989

Phase II Office Building
Village Shirlington
Arlington, VA
The Oliver Carr Company, 1989

901 E Street[14]
Washington, DC
Quadrangle Development Corporation
1989

Washington Tower
Pentagon City
Arlington, VA
Rose Associates, Inc., 1989

Bank of Baltimore Building[15]
Baltimore, MD
Manekin Corporation/Clark
Enterprises Inc., 1989

Physicians Pavilion at Owings Mills[16]
Owings Mills, MD
Greater Baltimore Medical Center
1989

Tower City Office Building
Cleveland, OH
Forest City Enterprises, 1990

10

11

12

13

14

15

16

Computer Sciences Corporation
Phase III—Virginia Technology Center
Falls Church, VA
Computer Sciences Corporation and
Cadillac Fairview Urban Development
Inc., 1990

**L-1 Research & Development Building at
University Center**
Loudoun County, VA
The Charles E. Smith Companies, 1990

Courthouse Square
Towson, MD
The KMS Group and the First
National Bank of Maryland, 1990

Reston Phase One Office Buildings
Reston, VA
Reston Town Center Associates, 1990

Far East Trade Center
Office Building
Washington, DC
The Alex. Conroy Company; Melvin
Simon & Associates, Inc., 1990

Two Democracy Plaza
Bethesda, MD
The Charles E. Smith Companies, The
Artery Organization, and
Camalier/Davis Families, 1990

Bank One Center[17]
Cleveland, OH
John W. Galbreath & Co., 1991

Bank of Trade Center
Los Angeles, CA
Hip Hing Holdings, The Mellon
Company, 1991

Allstate Carillon[18]
Tampa, FL
Allstate Insurance Company, 1991

First Union Center
Fort Lauderdale, FL
The Regency Group, 1991

IBM/Kodak Operations Center[19]
Rochester, NY
Integrated Systems Solutions Corp., a
wholly owned subsidiary of IBM, 1991

The Acacia Group
Washington, DC, 1991

**B1 & B2 Buildings at Fairfax County
Government Center Corporate Park**
Fairfax, VA
The Smith/Artery Partnership, 1992

*Commerce Place
Baltimore, MD
Harlan-KDC Associates, 1992

Corporate Park at Government Center
A2 and A3 Buildings
Fairfax County, VA
The Smith/Artery Partnership

*Fairfax County Government Center
Fairfax, VA
The Charles E. Smith Companies/The
Artery Organization, 1992

**British Aerospace North American
Headquarters**[20]
Herndon, VA
British Aerospace and the Mark
Winkler Company, 1992

525 B Street
San Diego, CA
Tishman Speyer Properties, 1992

Eletropaulo
São Paulo, Brazil
Lafonte Participacoes, 1993

Crocker Executive Center[21]
Boca Raton, FL
Crocker & Company, 1993

The Riverside
Jacksonville, FL
The Regency Group, 1993

Star Diamond Center
Taipei, Taiwan
Sing/Tran Investment Company, 1993

Suluh Fashion Center
Jakarta, Indonesia
PT Rismar
Transindo Nasional, 1993

17

18

19

20

Kuningan Office Tower
Jakarta, Indonesia
Confidential, 1993

Empire Place
Jakarta, Indonesia
Lippoland Development, 1993

IBM Command Center[22]
Boulder, CO
Integrated Systems Solutions
Corporation, a wholly owned subsidiary
of IBM, 1994

Sinar Mas Plaza
Jakarta, Indonesia
Sinar Mas Group, 1994

*Sudirman Tower
Jakarta, Indonesia
Lippoland Development, 1995

Grand Kuningan A-9 Shop Offices
Jakarta, Indonesia
Abadi Guna Papan, 1995

201 East Pine
Orlando, FL
Heitman Properties Ltd, 1995

Textile Trade Mart
Taegu, South Korea
Daewoo Corporation, 1995

*TNB Corporate Tower
Kuala Lumpur, Malaysia
Tanaga Nasional Berhad, 1995

Senayan Square[23]
Jakarta, Indonesia
Kajima Corporation, 1996

Dirksen, Hart, and Russell
Senate Office Building Renovations
Washington, DC
Architect of the Capitol, 1996

Cannon and Longworth
House Office Building Renovations
Washington, DC
Architect of the Capitol, 1996

1200 New Hampshire Avenue
Washington, DC
Heitman Properties Ltd, 1996

Tver Universal Bank
Tver, Russia
Hudson Partners, 1996

Shanghai Insurance Tower
Shanghai, China
Shanghai Insurance Co., Shanghai
Design Institute of Light Industry

Golden Key Office Tower
Jakarta, Indonesia
PT Sentraprima Metropolitan, 1996

1333 New Hampshire Avenue
Washington, DC
The JBG Companies, 1996

*Gentor Oficinas Corporativas
Monterrey, Neuvo Leon, Mexico
Grupo Gentor, 1996

T. Rowe Price Financial Center[24]
Owings Mills, MD
T. Rowe Price Associates, Inc., 1997

*Block 68
Beirut, Lebanon
Solidere, 1997

*Centro Empresarial Monterrey
Monterrey, Mexico
ICA Associadas, 1998

*SABIC Headquarters
Riyadh, Saudi Arabia
Saudi Arabian Basic Industries
Corporation, 1998

*Warsaw Business Center
Warsaw, Poland
Daewoo Corporation, 1998

**Saitama National Government Buildings
(Saitama Koiki Godochosha)**[25]
Saitama Prefecture, Japan
Ministry of Construction, Kanto
Regional Bureau, 1999

21

22

23

24

25

Public Sector

Annapolis State Office Building
Annapolis, MD
State of Maryland, 1956

Fort Detrick Clinical Research Facility
Frederick, MD
US Army Corps of Engineers,
Baltimore District, 1970

HEW Federal Office Complex Master Plan
Washington, DC
US Department of Health,
Education, and Welfare, 1971

Aberdeen Proving Ground
Aberdeen, MD
US Army Corps of Engineers,
Baltimore District, 1975

Walter Reed Army Medical Center
Washington, DC
US Army Corps of Engineers,
Baltimore District, 1975

Board of Education Building
Annapolis, MD
Anne Arundel County, 1975

**Edward A. Garmatz Federal Building
and US Courthouse**[1]
Baltimore, MD
US General Services Administration,
1977

**National Naval Medical Center
Development Plan**
Bethesda, MD
Naval Facilities Engineering Command,
Chesapeake Division, 1978

Embassy of Saudi Arabia
Washington, DC
The Kingdom of Saudi Arabia, 1984

French Chancery
Washington, DC
The Republic of France, 1985

Brooke Army Medical Center
San Antonio, TX
US Army Corps of Engineers,
Fort Worth District, 1985

Saudi Arabian Chancery[2]
Washington, DC
The Kingdom of Saudi Arabia, 1985

US Embassy Facilities Evaluation
Belgrade, Yugoslavia
US Department of State,
Office of Foreign Buildings Operations
1987

US Capitol Perimeter Security Study
Washington, DC
Architect of the Capitol, 1987

Building 111, US Navy Yard[3]
Washington, DC
Naval Facilities Engineering Command,
Chesapeake Division, 1988

Defense Intelligence Agency
Analysis Center Expansion
Bolling AFB, Washington, DC
Naval Facilities Engineering Command,
Chesapeake Division
Joint Venture Partners: HOK and
DMJM, Pending

Parking Garage US Navy Yard
Washington, DC
Naval Facilities Engineering Command,
Chesapeake Division
1988 (Phase 1) 1990 (Phase 2)

Charles L. Benton Jr. Office Building
Baltimore, MD
Trustees for the City of Baltimore, 1988

Multi-Purpose Office Building
Montgomery County, MD
US Army Corps of Engineers, Baltimore
District, 1989

Department of Veterans Affairs
Facility Development Plans
Fort Howard, MD; Hampton, VA;
Asheville, NC; and Lebanon, PA
US Department of Veterans Affairs
1989–1994

Indefinite Delivery Contract
US Department of State
Various locations worldwide
US Department of State,
Office of Foreign Buildings Operations
1991–96

Classified Operations Facility
Location withheld
US Army Corps of Engineers,
Baltimore District, 1992

NASA Indefinite Quantity Contract
Greenbelt, MD, and other US locations
National Aeronautics and Space
Administration, 1992–96

Indefinite Quantity Contract
Federal Bureau of Investigation
Various locations nationwide
Federal Bureau of Investigation
1992–97

*Fairfax County Government Center[4]
Fairfax, VA
The Smith/Artery Partnership, 1992

**IRS Office Consolidation Project for the
National Office**
Metropolitan Washington, DC area
Department of the Treasury, Internal
Revenue Service, 1993

*Embassy of Singapore[5]
Washington, DC
Republic of Singapore, 1993

**Arts & Industries Building Renovation
Master Plan**
Smithsonian Institution
Washington, DC
Smithsonian Institution, 1993

'Castle' Building Renovation Master Plan
Smithsonian Institution
Washington, DC
Smithsonian Institution, 1994

US Ambassador's Residence[6]
Bangkok, Thailand
US Department of State, Office of
Foreign Buildings Operations
1994 (design)

Federal Correctional Institution[7]
Cumberland, MD
US Department of Justice,
Federal Bureau of Prisons, 1994

**The European Union Delegation of the
European Commission**
Washington, DC, 1994

National Maritime Intelligence Center[8]
Suitland, MD
Naval Facilities Engineering Command,
Chesapeake Division
Joint Venture Partners,: HOK and
DMJM, 1994

*US Capitol Visitor Center[9]
Washington, DC
Architect of the Capitol, 1995

*Embassy of Sweden[10]
Washington, DC
The Government of Sweden, 1995

*US Ambassador's Residence Renovation[11]
Tokyo, Japan
US Department of State, Office of
Foreign Buildings Operations, 1995

**Health Care Financing Administration
Headquarters**[12]
Baltimore, MD
General Services Administration and
Boston Properties, Inc., 1995

Classified Government Agency
Headquarters Facility and
Consolidation Contract
Location withheld, 1995

**Classified Government Agency
NPIC Task Order Contract**
Location withheld, 1995

US Army Research Laboratory[13]
Adelphi, MD
US Army Corps of Engineers,
Baltimore District
Joint Venture Partner: Anderson
DeBartolo Pan, Inc., 1996

US Embassy Complex[14]
Bayan, Kuwait
US Department of State, Office of
Foreign Buildings Operations, 1996

*US Ambassador's Residence
Bayan, Kuwait
US Department of State, Office of
Foreign Buildings Operations, 1996

National Cancer Institute
Frederick, MD
National Cancer Institute, 1996

6

7

8

9

10

Dirksen, Hart, and Russell
Senate Office Building Renovations
Washington, DC
Architect of the Capitol, 1996

Cannon and Longworth
House Office Building Renovations
Washington, DC
Architect of the Capitol, 1996

George H. Fallon Federal Building
Baltimore, MD
US General Services Administration
Region III, 1997

Classified Government Agencies
Backfill Master Plan and
Implementation
Location withheld, 1998
Headquarters Facility, Virginia
General Services Administration

*Headquarters Facility
Virginia
General Services Administration

**US Customs Service and Interstate
Commerce Commission**
Connecting Wing Buildings Complex
Modernization
Washington, DC
General Services Administration, 2000

Indonesian Consulate Offices
Hong Kong
PT Dewata Wibawa

US Naval Academy, Bancroft Hall
Annapolis, MD
Naval Facilities Engineering Command,
Engineering Field Activity Chesapeake,
2002

**General Services Administration
Task Order Contract**
Various locations
General Services Administration
ongoing

Residential

*Montgomery Village[1]
Montgomery County, MD
Kettler Brothers, Inc., 1970

North Avenue Housing
Baltimore, MD
City of Baltimore, 1972

Brickell Key
Miami, FL
Swire Properties Inc. and Cheezem
Development, 1979

Lakeport[2]
Reston, VA
Castro-Holdsworth Associates, 1985

Harbor Point
Reston, VA
Castro-Holdsworth Associates, 1985

*State-Thomas Area Plan
Dallas, TX
Friends of State-Thomas and
the City of Dallas, 1986

Thomas Street Housing
Dallas, TX
Street Investments, 1987

Clove Leaf Germantown Center
Montgomery County, MD
The Manekin Corporation, 1988

South Bluffs
Memphis, TN
Glacier Park Company and
The Henry Turley Company, 1988

*Harbor Town, Mud Island
Memphis, TN
Island Property Associates, 1988

Heritage Landing Development Plan
Minneapolis, MN
Glacier Park, 1989

EuroDisney Multi-Family Housing
Marne La Vallée, France
Lincoln Properties, 1990

Kishiwada Port Redevelopment
Kishiwada, Japan
Kishiwada Port Development
Corporation, 1991

11

12

13

14

1

2

Block 81
Long Beach, CA
Janss Corporation, 1991

Hunter's Ridge at Las Colinas
Las Colinas, TX
Urban Investment and
Development Co., 1991

Via Ranch
Houston, TX
American General Investment
Corporation, 1991

Moreno Highlands[3]
Moreno Valley, CA
Moreno Highlands Company, 1991

Les Lacs Special District Plan
Addison, TX
Town of Addison, 1991

Cinco Ranch
Houston, TX
Cinco Ranch Development
Corporation, 1991

**Baldhead Island Resort/
Commercial Center**
Baldhead Island, SC
Baldhead Island Management Inc., 1991

Proyecto San Jeronimo
Monterrey, Nuevo Leon, Mexico
Progresso, 1992

Obregon New Community Master Plan[4]
Obregon, Sonora, Mexico
Fideicomiso Progreso, 1992

Private Residence
Washington, DC, 1992

Pine Square/Pacific Court[5]
Long Beach, CA
Janss Corporation, 1992

*Euro Val d'Oise
Roissy, France
Euro Val d'Oise Association, 1992

Falling Waters Residential
Baton Rouge, LA
Royal Marque Company, Ltd, 1992

Fieldstone Farms
Franklin, TN
American General Land Development
Corp., 1992

Bonah Indah Gardens
Jakarta, Indonesia
Bonauli Real Estate, 1992

Bali Pecatu
Bali, Indonesia
Putrisekar Maharani, 1993

Ciawi Country Club
Bogor, Indonesia
PT Pamada Jaya, 1993

Simpruk Residential Towers
Jakarta, Indonesia
PT Trireska Lestari, 1993

*Shae-Zee Island
Taipei, Taiwan
Department of City Planning,
City of Taipei, 1993

Sogo Pernas Centre
Kuala Lumpur, Malaysia
Taisei Corporation, 1993

Sui Bao Tower
Shenzhen, China
Shirble Holdings (Shenzen) Industrial,
Ltd, 1994

Las Mitras New Community Planning
Monterrey, N.L., Mexico
Protexa Corporation, 1994

Club City/Makuhari Mid-Rise Housing
Tokyo, Japan
Shimizu Corporation, 1994

Tangerang Garden Estate
Jakarta, Indonesia
PT Ometraco Realty, 1994

3

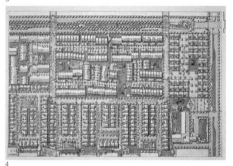

4

5

6

Senayan Square Housing
Jakarta, Indonesia
Kajima Overseas Asia, 1994

Bumimas Towers[6]
Jakarta, Indonesia
Bumimas Development Corp., 1994

The Quantum
Jakarta, Indonesia
PT Dewata Wibawa, 1994

Wanakerta Residential Master Plan[7]
Jakarta, Indonesia
PT Sinar Puspapersada, 1994

Jakarta Golf Village[8]
Kemayoran, Jakarta, Indonesia
Megacity Development Corporation
1995

Omni Marco Polo Hotel Mixed-Use Center
Wuhan, China
Golden Resources Ltd, 1995

Four Seasons Regent Residences
Jakarta, Indonesia
PT Dewata Wibawa, 1995

*Dalian New City Center
Dalian, Liaoning Province, China
Dalian Economic and Technical
Development Zone, 1995

Grande Family Estate
Surabaya, Indonesia
PT Dharmala Land, 1996

Grogol Expansion of Citraland
Jakarta, Indonesia
Ciputra Group, 1996

*Rama III
Bangkok, Thailand
Estate Development Company Ltd
and Central Department Stores, 1997

Grand Kuningan[9]
Jakarta, Indonesia
Abadi Guna Papan, 1997

Hume Parcel No. 4 Condominium Towers
Singapore
City Developments Ltd, 1997

Tianjin Mixed Use Project
Tianjin, China
Tianjin Sanloon Enterprise
Development Co., 1997

American Place
Shanghai, China
KDG Kennard Design Group, 1997

Gold Coast Elevation Study
Tuen Mun, Hong Kong
Sino Land, 1999

Punta Fuego Resort
Luzon, Philippines
Landco, 1999

Cebu Talisay Residential Master Plan
Cebu, Philippines
Landco, 1999

Filinvest Residential Towers
Alabang, Metro Manila, Philippines
Moldex Realty, 1999

Roxas Blvd Residential Tower
Manila, Philippines
Moldex Realty, 1999

Retail Centers & Department Stores

Harundale Mall
Glen Burnie, MD
The Rouse Company, 1958

Belair Shopping Center
Bowie, MD
Levitt & Son Inc., 1960

The Mall
Louisville, KY
The Rouse Company, 1962

Paramus Park Mall[1]
Paramus, NJ
The Rouse Company, 1972

Abraham & Straus
Paramus Park Mall
Paramus Park, NJ
Abraham & Straus, 1974

7

8

9

White Flint Mall[2]
Rockville, MD
The Lerner Company, 1977

Bloomingdale's
White Flint Mall
Bethesda, MD
Bloomingdale's, 1977

Beachwood Place
Cleveland, OH
The Rouse Company, 1978

Valley Hills Mall
Hickory, NC
Cadillac Fairview Shopping Centers
US, Ltd, 1978

Abraham & Straus
Monmouth Mall
Monmouth, NJ
Abraham & Straus, 1978

Lazarus
Washington Square
Indianapolis, IN
Lazarus, 1978

Hechinger Center
Washington, DC
Hechinger Co., 1979

Lazarus
Greenwood Mall
Indianapolis, IN
Lazarus, 1979

Shannon Mall
Atlanta, GA
Cadillac Fairview Shopping Centers,
Ltd, 1980

Greenspoint Mall
Houston, TX
Federated Stores Realty Inc., 1980

North Hills Mall (expansion 1984)
Fort Worth, TX
Federated Stores Realty Inc., 1980

Abraham & Straus
The Galleria
White Plains, NY
Abraham & Straus, 1980

Sears
Fair Oaks Mall
Fairfax, VA
Sears Roebuck & Company, 1980

Abraham & Straus
Short Hills Mall
Short Hills, NJ
Abraham & Straus, 1980

Arnot Mall (renovation)[3]
Elmira, NY
Arnot Realty Company, 1981

White Marsh Mall
White Marsh, MD
The Rouse Company, 1981

Stratford Square[4]
Bloomingdale, IL
Urban Investment Company, 1981

Collin Creek
Plano, TX
Federated Stores Realty Inc., 1981

Hunt Valley Mall
Hunt Valley, MD
Kravco Corporation, 1981

Hutzler's
White Marsh Mall
White Marsh, MD
Hutzler Bros. Co., 1981

Abraham & Straus
King of Prussia Mall
King of Prussia, PA
Abraham & Straus, 1981

Sears
Arnot Mall
Elmira, NY
Sears Roebuck & Company, 1981

Sears
Huntington Mall
Barboursville, WV
Sears Roebuck & Company, 1981

Foothills Mall
Tucson, AZ
Federated Stores Realty Inc., 1982

Willow Grove Park
Abington Township, PA
Federated Stores Realty Inc., and
Richard I. Rubin Company, 1982

Abraham & Straus
Willow Grove Park
Willow Grove, PA
Abraham & Straus, 1982

Strawbridge & Clothier
Burlington Center
Burlington, NJ
Strawbridge & Clothier, 1982

The Citadel (expansion)
Colorado Springs, CO
The Rouse Company, 1983

Gwinnett Place[5]
Atlanta, GA
Cadillac Fairview Shopping Centers US,
Ltd, 1983

Valley View Mall (expansion/renovation)
Dallas, TX
LaSalle Street Fund Inc., 1983

Saks Fifth Avenue
Canal Place
New Orleans, LA
Batus Retail Division of Saks Fifth
Avenue, 1983

Strawbridge & Clothier
Concord Mall
New Castle, DE
Strawbridge & Clothier, 1983

Bloomingdale's
Valley View Mall
Dallas, TX
Bloomingdale's, 1983

West Oaks Mall
Houston, TX
Federated Stores Realty Inc., 1984

Northpark
Ridgeland, MS
Cadillac Fairview Shopping Centers US,
Ltd, 1984

South Bay Galleria[6]
Redondo Beach, CA
Forest City Enterprises, 1985

The Esplanade[7]
New Orleans, LA
Cadillac Fairview Shopping Centers US,
Ltd, 1985

West Town Mall (renovation)
Knoxville, TN
The RREEF Funds and
Carter & Associates, 1985

Thalhimers
Northwoods Mall
Charleston, SC
Thalhimers, 1985

Thalhimers
Valley View Mall
Roanoke, VA
Thalhimers, 1985

Town Center at Cobb
Cobb County, GA
Cadillac Fairview Shopping Centers US,
Ltd, 1986

Polo Park
Winnipeg, Manitoba, Canada
Cadillac Fairview Shopping Centers
Canada, Ltd, 1986

Woodbine Centre[8]
Toronto, Ontario, Canada
Cadillac Fairview/JMB Federated, 1986

Owings Mills Town Center
Owings Mills, MD
The Rouse Company, 1986

Promenade
Toronto, Ontario, Canada
Cadillac Fairview/JMB Federated, 1986

Town Center at Boca Raton (expansion)[9]
Boca Raton, FL
JMB/Federated Realty Associates, Ltd
1986

Ballston Common[10]
Arlington, VA
May Centers and Forest City Rental
Properties, 1986

Orlando Fashion Square (renovation)
Orlando, FL
Leonard L. Farber Inc., 1987

Portage Place[11]
Winnipeg, Manitoba, Canada
Cadillac Fairview/JMB Federated, 1987

South Gate (renovation)
Sarasota, FL
Equity Properties and Development
Company, 1987

The CrossRoads of San Antonio (addition)
San Antonio, TX
The Lehndorff Group, 1987

Princeton Market Fair[12]
Princeton, NJ
JMB/Federated Realty, 1987

Blue Bonnet Mall
Baton Rouge, LA
Cadillac Fairview Shopping Centers US,
Ltd, 1987

Newport Centre
Jersey City, NJ
Melvin Simon & Associates, Inc., 1987

Manhattan Town Center
Manhattan, KS
Forest City Development Group, 1988

Greenbriar Mall (renovation)
Atlanta, GA
Lehndorff Management (USA) Ltd
1988

Penn Square Mall (renovation)
Oklahoma City, OK
JMB/Federated, 1988

**Fashion Mall at Keystone at the Crossing
(addition)**
Indianapolis, IN
Duke Associates, 1988

Coliseum Mall (renovation and expansion)
Hampton, VA
Mall Properties Inc., 1988

*Tysons Corner Center
McLean, VA
Lehndorff Management (USA) Ltd
1988

Darling Harbourside[13]
Sydney, Australia
Merlin International Properties
(Australia) Pty. Ltd and The Enterprise
Development Company, 1988

IKEA[14]
White Marsh Mall
White Marsh, MD
IKEA, 1988

Pavilion Saks Fifth Avenue[15]
Houston, TX
Kenneth H. Hughes Interests and
Alrich, Eastman, Waltch, 1989

Hawthorn Center (renovation)
Vernon Hills, IL
JMB Properties Company and The
O'Connor Group, 1989

The Plaza at West Covina[16]
West Covina, CA
May Centers; Shulman Company, 1989

Galleria Orlando
Orlando, FL
The Prudential; Major Realty Corp. and
Alan Squitieri, 1989

The Shops at the Bellevue
Philadelphia, PA
Richard I. Rubin & Co., Inc., 1989

A&S Plaza[17]
New York, NY
Melvin Simon & Associates, Inc.,
Silverstein Properties, Inc. and
Zeckendorf Company, Inc., 1989

Neiman Marcus[18]
Tysons Corner II
Tysons Corner, VA
Neiman Marcus, 1989

Burdines at The Gardens
The Gardens Mall
Palm Beach Gardens, FL
Burdines, 1989

14

15

16

17

18

19

Olssons Books•Records[19]
Washington, DC
Olssons Books•Records, 1989

Strawbridge & Clothier[20]
King of Prussia Mall
King of Prussia, PA
Strawbridge & Clothier, 1989

Strawbridge & Clothier
(facade renovation)
Willow Grove Park
Willow Grove, PA
Strawbridge & Clothier, 1989

Nashville Fashion Galleria
(renovation/expansion)
Nashville, TN
Cadillac Fairview Shopping Centers US,
Ltd, and Belz Enterprises, 1990

Christiana Mall
(renovation/expansion)
Wilmington, DE
Richard I. Rubin & Co., Inc., 1990

Hamilton Eaton Centre
Hamilton, Ontario, Canada
Cadillac Fairview and Eaton Properties
1990

Far East Trade Center
Washington, DC
Melvin Simon & Associates, Inc. and
The Conroy Company, 1990

Tiffany & Co.[21]
Philadelphia, PA
Tiffany & Co., 1990

Neiman Marcus at Cherry Creek
Cherry Creek Mall
Denver, CO
Neiman Marcus, 1990

Armoire
Newport Beach, CA
Armoire with Donohue Schriber, 1990

Brea Mall[22]
Brea, CA
Corporate Property Investors, 1990

*Farmers Market at Atrium Court
Newport Beach, CA
Irvine Retail Properties Co., 1990

Chadstone Centre[23]
Melbourne, Australia
The Gandel Group of Companies, 1990

Tucson Mall (renovation)
Tucson, AZ
Forest City Enterprises, 1991

Ward Parkway Mall
(renovation)
Kansas City, MO
The O'Connor Group, 1991

Montgomery Mall[24]
(renovation/expansion)
Bethesda, MD
CenterMark Properties, Inc., 1991

Livingston Mall[25]
(renovation/expansion)
Livingston, NJ
Corporate Property Investors, 1991

Erin Mills Town Centre[26]
Mississauga, Ontario, Canada
Cadillac Fairview Corporation Ltd/Erin
Mills Development Corp., 1991

One Schaumburg Place
Northbrook, IL
The Tucker Companies, 1991

*Menlo Park
(renovation/expansion)
Edison Township, NJ
The O'Connor Group, 1991

Cumberland Mall
(renovation)
Atlanta, GA
Yarmouth Group, 1991

*Towson Town Center
(expansion/renovation)
Towson, MD
The Hahn Company, 1991

*The Courtyard Shops of Encino
Encino, CA
Security Pacific Corporation, 1991

20

21

22

23

24

Hudson's Bay Centre
Hudson's Bay Centre
Edmonton, Alberta, Canada
Stewart, Green Properties Ltd, 1991

Northbrook Court
(renovation)
Northbrook, IL
Grosvenor International (Atlantic)
Limited, 1992

*Valencia Town Center[27]
Valencia, CA
Valencia Town Center Assoc., LP; JMB
Retail Properties Ltd; and The Newhall
Land and Farming Co., 1992

Promenade at Woodland Hills
Woodlands Hills, CA
The O'Connor Group, 1992

Harvard Place at Jamboree Centre
Irvine, CA
The Irvine Co., 1992

Plaza del Caribe
Ponce, Puerto Rico
Empresas Fonalledas, 1992

A&S Roosevelt Field Mall[28]
Garden City, Long Island, NY
Federated Department Stores,
Inc./A&S Division, 1992

New City
Higashi Totsuka, Japan
Kumagai Gumi, 1992

Goshono Town Center
Akita, Japan
Aeon Kosan, 1993

Canal Walk Cafes at Georgetown Park[29]
Washington, DC
JMB Retail Properties, Inc., 1993

*Farmers Market
Los Angeles, CA
Gilmore Company and JMB Retail
Properties, Inc., 1993

Sogo Pernas Centre
Kuala Lumpur, Malaysia
Taisei Corporation, 1993

Willowbrook Mall
(renovation)
Houston, TX
The Yarmouth Group, 1993

Hillsdale Mall
(renovation)
San Mateo, CA
Bohannan Development Co., 1993

*Roosevelt Field Mall
(renovation/expansion)
Garden City, NY
Corporate Property Investors, 1993

*The Boulevard
(expansion/renovation)
Las Vegas, NV
MEPC American Properties, Inc., 1993

Shopper's World
Framingham, MA
Melvin Simon & Associates, Inc., 1993

Brunswick Square
(renovation/expansion)
Brunswick, NJ
The Edward J. DeBartolo Co., 1993

Ram Intra
Bangkok, Thailand
Central Pattana Development Co. Ltd
1993

Town Center at Boca Raton
(expansion)
Boca Raton, FL
Corporate Property Investors, 1994

Fort Worth Town Center
(renovation)
Fort Worth, TX
Weitzman Properties and Citicorp, 1994

Crabtree Valley Mall
(renovation)
Raleigh, NC
Crabtree Valley Mall Associates, 1994

*Lenox Square[30]
(renovation/expansion)
Atlanta, GA
Corporate Property Investors, 1994

25 26

27

28

29

Shopping Center Iguatemi
São Paulo, Brazil
La Fonte Trading Co., 1994

West Hills Regional Centre
Calgary, Alberta, Canada
Stewart Green Properties, 1994

*The Galleria Morley[31]
Perth, Australia
Coles Myer Properties Ltd and Colonial
Mutual Life Assurance Society Ltd, 1994

Seacon Square
Bangkok, Thailand
Seacon Development Group, 1994

Hecht's
Northgate Mall
Durham, NC
May Design & Construction Co., 1994

Kaufmann's Home Store
McKinley Mall
Hamburg, NY
May Design & Construction Co., 1994

The Shops at The Watergate
Washington, DC
The JBG Companies, 1994

Famous-Barr Men's/Home Store
(new entrance)
Northpark Mall
Joplin, MO
May Design & Construction Co., 1994

Plaza Indonesia Renovation
Jakarta, Indonesia
Plaza Indonesia Realty Ltd, 1994

Sears Repositioning Program
Reno, NV
San Bruno, CA
Santa Monica, CA
Bakersfield, CA
Fresno, CA
Northridge, CA
Athens, GA
Davenport, IA
Schaumberg, IL
Jackson, MS
Greensboro, NC
Mesquite, TX
Valley View Mall, Dallas, TX
Brookfield, WI
Glendale, WI
Milwaukee, WI

Greendale, WI
Sears San Agustin, Mexico
Sears Anahuac, Mexico[32]
Sears Merchandise Group
1994–99

*Centro Comercial Diagonal Mar
Barcelona, Spain
The Prime Group, 1995

*The Westchester[33]
White Plains, NY
The O'Connor Group and Nomura
Real Estate USA, 1995

*Brandon Town Center
Tampa, FL
Urban Retail Properties Co. formerly
JMB Retail Properties Company, 1995

Filene's
Marlborough Mall
Berlin, MA
May Design & Construction Co., 1995

Filene's
Waterbury Towne Center
Waterbury, CT
May Design & Construction Co., 1995

*Eastland Shopping Centre
Melbourne, Australia
Coles Myer Properties, Ltd, 1995

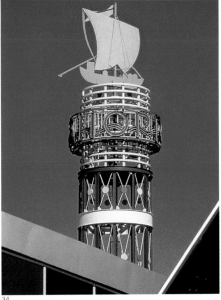

GAIA Shopping[34]
Vila Nova da GAIA, Portugal
Grupo Sonae, 1995

*Northridge Fashion Center[35]
Northridge, CA
MEPC American Properties Inc., 1995

Hecht's
Manassas Mall
Manassas, VA
May Design & Construction Co., 1995

Greenbelt Mall & Park Square 2
Makati, Metro Manila, Philippines
Ayala Land, Inc., 1995

Filinvest Corporate City
Alabang, Metro Manila, Philippines
Filinvest Land, Inc., 1995

Alabang Town Center
Manila, Philippines
Ayala Land, Inc., 1995

Ayala Center
Makati, Metro Manila, Philippines
Ayala Land, Inc., 1995

*****Centro Augusta**
Zaragosa, Spain
Centro Comerciales Continente, 1995

Grace Bros. Department Store[36]
Grace Bros. Centre
Sydney, Australia
Coles Myer Properties Ltd, 1996

Beachwood Mall (renovation)
Cleveland, OH
The Rouse Co., 1996

Tacoma Mall
Tacoma, WA
DeBartolo Properties Management,
Inc., 1996

Metro Centro
San Salvadore
Inversiones Roble, 1996

Multi Plaza
Costa Rica
Inversiones Roble, 1996

Fort Worth Outlet Square
Fort Worth, TX
Tandy Corporation, 1996

First Colony Mall
Houston, TX
Gerald D. Hines Interests, 1996

The Avenue at White Marsh[37]
White Marsh, MD
Nottingham Properties, 1996

Target/Cairns Centre
Cairns, Queensland, Australia
Coles Myer Properties Ltd, 1996

Myer/Toowoomba Shopping Centre
Toowoomba, Queensland, Australia
Coles Myer Properties Ltd, 1996

Robinson/May
Galleria at Sunset
Henderson, NV
May Design & Construction Co., 1996

*****Rama III**
Bangkok, Thailand
Estate Development Company Ltd and
Central Department Stores, 1997

*****Centro Oberhausen**
Oberhausen, Germany
Neue Mitte Projektenwicklung GmbH
1997

Norte Shopping
Matoshinos, Portugal
Grupo Sonae, 1997

Wolfchase Galleria
Memphis, TN
Urban Retail Properties Co., 1997

Tuen Mun Town Center
Kowloon, Hong Kong
Sino Land, 1997

Clarke Quay Retail Project
Singapore
Clarke Quay Pte. Ltd/DBS Land, 1997

Rama IX Mall
Bangkok, Thailand
Mall Group, 1998

Bandra-Kurla Shopping Center
India
Kalpa Taru Construction Overseas
Pte., Ltd, 1998

Braehead Park
Glasgow, Scotland
Braehead Park Ltd, a joint venture of
Marks & Spencer plc, J. Sainsbury plc
and CSC, 1998

Citrus Park Mall
Tampa, FL
Urban Retail Properties, 1998

36

37

38

39

Paramount Plaza
Manila, Philippines
Paramount Holdings Equities Inc.

Penang/Gurney Road Project
Penang, Malaysia
Metro Holdings Ltd, 1998

Amcorp Plaza
Kuala Lumpur, Malaysia
Melawangi Sdn. Bhd., 1998

Myer
Myer Centre
Melbourne, Australia
Coles Myer Properties Ltd

Fenix Park[38]
Genk, Belgium
The Stadium Group, 1999

GUM 2000[39]
Moscow, Russia
International Realty Investors,
Trade House GUM, 2000

Transportation

Washington Metro-Federal Center and Capitol South Stations
Washington, DC
Washington Metropolitan Area Transit Authority, 1976

Charles Center Metro[1]
Baltimore, MD
Baltimore Mass Transit Administration
1983

Newport City PATH Station
Jersey City, NJ
Port Authority of New York and New Jersey and Newport City Development Company Design Collaborative, 1985

Takamatsu
Takamatsu, Japan
Confidential, 1990

***Universal Starway**
Universal City, CA
MCA/Universal Studios, 1991

Worcester Airport[2]
Worcester, MA
City of Worcester, 1993

***Miyazaki Station**[3,4]
Kyushu, Japan
Japan Rail Kyushu, 1993

Dresden Airport[5]
Dresden, Germany
Hochtief Projektentwicklung GmbH
1993

Bangkok Bus Terminal
Bangkok, Thailand, 1995

MCA Backlot Tram Facility[6]
Hollywood, CA
Universal Studios, 1995

Chek Lap Kok Airport
Retail Areas
Hong Kong
Foster Asia, 1997

Dallas/Fort Worth International Airport
Dallas, TX
Dallas/Fort Worth International
Airport, 1997

Urban Design and Master Planning (1970–present)

Fort Totten Study
Washington, DC
Cafritz Company, 1970

Loudoun County Planned Community
Leesburg, VA
Levitt & Sons, 1970

Squantum Point
Squantum, MA
Cabot, Cabot, & Forbes, 1971

Plan for Downtown Jacksonville[1]
Jacksonville, FL
Jacksonville Area Planning Board, 1971

Largo Town Center
Largo, MD
Northampton Corporation, 1972

Spring Park
Dallas, TX
Nasher Properties, Inc., 1973–1985

Seton Properties
Baltimore, MD
Rivkon/Carson, Inc.
Department of Housing and
Community Development, 1974

Union Station
Development Concept
Nashville, TN
Union Square Ltd, 1977

South Lakes Village Center
Reston, VA
Reston Land Corp., 1978

Miami Town Center
Miami, FL
Cadillac Fairview Shopping Centers, Ltd
and Homart Development Co., 1979

Charlotte Central Area Plan[2]
Charlotte, NC
Department of Urban
Development, City of Charlotte, 1980

Burlington Square
Burlington, VT
American Metropolitan Development
Corp., 1981

*Cincinnati 2000[3]
Cincinnati, OH
City of Cincinnati, 1981

Reading Downtown Development Plan[4]
Reading, PA
City of Reading, Bureau of Planning
1981

Cambridge Office and Research Park
Cambridge, MA
Forest City Enterprises, 1982

Garrison Channel Development
Tampa, FL
Major Realty Corporation, 1982

Mile High Land Project[5]
Denver, CO
Mile High Land Associates;
Glacier Park Co.; Miller, Klutznick,
Davis, Gray Co.; Urban Investment and
Development Co., 1983

Hunters Ridge
Las Colinas, TX
Urban Investment and Development
Co., 1983

Rocky Hill
Rocky Hill, CT
Equity Ventures Incorporated, 1984

Jones Block Development
Kansas City, MO
Cross Town Development, 1984

Lincolnwood
Evanston, IL
Melvin Simon & Associates, Inc., 1984

Potomac Place
Arlington, VA
City of Richmond and Frederick
and Potomac Railroad, 1984

Lit Block
Philadelphia, PA
Richard I. Rubin & Co., Inc., 1984

The Highlands of Arlington
Jones Block Development
Kansas City, MO
Cross Town Development, 1984

189 Peachtree Street
Atlanta, GA
JMB/Federated Realty Associates, Ltd
1984

Charleston Town Center
Pedestrian Way
Improvement Guidelines
Charleston, WV
City of Charleston, 1985

Charleston Town Center
Forest City Enterprises
Charleston, WV, 1985

Plan for Downtown Arlington
Arlington, TX
City of Arlington, 1985

The Brandywine Center[6]
Wilmington, DE
Brandywine Raceway, 1985

Commercial Development Guidelines
Nassau Bay, TX
City of Nassau Bay, 1986

Fairview Park[7]
Fairfax County, VA
Cadillac Fairview Urban Development
1986

*State-Thomas Area Plan
Dallas, TX
Friends of State-Thomas and the City of
Dallas, 1986

Cowboys Center at Valley Ranch
Irving, TX
Halcyon, Ltd and Triland Development
Inc., 1986

Newport City[8]
Jersey City, NJ
Melvin Simon & Associates, Inc. and
The Lefrak Organization, 1986

*Reston Town Center[9]
Reston, VA
Reston Land Corporation and
Himmel/MKDG, 1982–86

San Jose 2010[10]
Comprehensive Plan
San Jose, CA
City of Jose, 1987

Providence Place at Capital Center
Providence, RI
The Conroy Company;
Melvin Simon & Associates Inc.;
Landow & Co., 1987

Allen Street Housing
Dallas, TX
Lehndorff USA, Inc., 1987

South Shore Harbour[11]
League City, TX
South Shore Harbour Development
Ltd, 1987

Centerpoint
Tempe, AZ
City of Tempe and DMB Associates, 1987

Myriad Gardens
Oklahoma City, OK
City of Oklahoma and Forest City
Enterprises, 1987

Flora Street
Dallas, TX
Billingsly Company, 1987

West End Urban Park
Dallas, TX
The West End Association, 1987

Comprehensive Planning Guide
Richardson, TX
City of Richardson, 1987

Thomas Street Housing
Dallas, TX
Street Investments, 1987

Synergy Park[12]
Richardson, TX
The University of Texas at Dallas, 1987

Piney Orchard Village Center
Odenton, MD
The Murphree Company, 1987

Park LaBrea
Los Angeles, CA
May Centers, Inc., 1987

Palmer Square North
Princeton, NJ
Collins Development Company, 1987

Queensport
Long Beach, CA
Wrather Corp., 1987

Downtown/Uptown[13]
West Palm Beach, FL
Rolfs/Paladin, 1987

Gulf Coast Center
Tampa, FL
JMB Realty Corp;
JMB/Federated Realty Associates;
Collier Enterprises, 1987

6

7

8

9

10

Lincoln West
New York, NY
The Trump Organization, 1987

University Place
New Haven, CT
University Place Associates, 1987

University of Dallas Campus Plan
Dallas, TX
University of Dallas, 1987

Inner Harbor East
Baltimore, MD
The Related Co., 1987

Brandywine Town Center
Wilmington, DE
Brandywine Raceway, 1988

Dadeland North
Miami, FL
The Green Companies, 1988

Boston Crossing
Boston, MA
Drucker Companies, 1988

Peabody Place
Memphis, TN
Belz Enterprises and
The City of Memphis, 1988

The Kentlands[14]
Gaithersburg, MD
Joseph Alfandre and Co., 1988

Onondaga Waterfront Plan
Syracuse, NY
City of Syracuse, 1988

Preston Center West
Dallas, TX
Preston Center Parking Authority, 1988

Wichita Downtown Revitalization Plan[15]
Wichita, KS
City of Wichita/Sedgwick County, 1988

Arlington Entertainment District Guidelines
Arlington, TX
City of Arlington, 1988

Downtown Plan
Lubbock, TX
City of Lubbock, 1988

Franklin Square
Syracuse, NY
City of Syracuse and Pyramid Co., 1988

Bryan and Cedar Area Plans
Dallas, TX
City of Dallas Coalition of Property and
Business Owners, 1988

Intown Housing Study
Dallas, TX
Central Dallas Association, 1988

South Bluffs
Memphis, TN
Glacier Park Company and the Henry
Turley Company, 1988

*Harbor Town, Mud Island
Memphis, TN
Island Property Associates, 1988

Matteson Village Center Study
Matteson, IL
City of Matteson and the National
Endowment for the Arts, 1988

Ryman Center
Nashville, TN
Matthews Company, 1988

Okayama Station Project
Okayama, Japan
Seibu Saison Group, 1988

Konterra Town Center[16]
Prince George's County, MD
Konterra Development Company, 1988

University Center[17]
Ashburne, VA
The Charles E. Smith Companies and
Michael Swerdlow Companies, 1988

Parkside Center
Farmers Branch, TX
Mobil Land Development Corporation
1988

11

12

13

Syracuse Redevelopment Plan
Syracuse, NY
The Pyramid Companies and the City
of Syracuse, 1989

Roanoke Downtown Development Plan
Roanoke, VA
Downtown Roanoke Inc., 1989

Park Central
Phoenix, AZ
The Lehndorff Group, 1989

**Northport Harbor Center
Development Plan**
Northport Harbor, FL
Deutsch/Ireland Co., 1989

Niseko West Valley Resort Community
Iwanai, Hokkaido, Japan
Tsukamoto Sangyo Co., Ltd, 1989

Heritage Landing Development Plan
Minneapolis, MN
Glacier Park, 1989

Giants Center Master Plan
Oceanport, NJ
Cali Associates, 1989

Gateway Village Center
Prince George's County, MD
Ratcliffe, Cali and Company, 1989

Fairfax Corner
Fairfax, VA
Sequoia Building Corporation, 1989

Columbus East Side
Mixed-Use Master Plan
Columbus, OH
DeBartolo, 1989

Cloverleaf Center Master Plan
Germantown, MD
Manekin Corporation, 1989

Izu Peninsula Resort[18]
Nishina, Japan
Alpha Resorts, Kajimam, 1989

CentrePark
Farmers Branch, TX
Centre Development, 1989

*Camden Yards Sports Complex
Baltimore, MD
Maryland Stadium Authority and
HOK Sports Facilities Group, 1989

Woodlands Metro Center
The Woodlands, TX
Mitchell Energy and Development
Corporation, 1990

Valley Ranch
Irving, TX
WJA Asset Management, 1990

University of Virginia
Health Sciences Master Plan
Charlottesville, VA
University of Virginia
Health Sciences Center, 1990

**Systems Command US Naval Master Plan
and Schematic Design**
Alexandria, VA
The Mark Winkler Company
and the GSA, 1990

**Rosslyn-Clarendon Metro Stations Urban
Design and Master Plan**
Urban Design and Master Plan
Rosslyn, VA
Arlington County Economic
Development Division, 1990

Richmond CBD Retail Strategy[19]
Richmond, VA
Economic Development, 1990

Rancho Mirage Town Center
Coachella Valley, CA
City of Rancho, Mirage and
Kenneth H. Hughes Interests, 1990

Raleigh Downtown Public Facilities Plan
Raleigh, NC
Downtown Raleigh Development
Corporation, 1990

President Street Corridor Study
Baltimore, MD
Whitman Requardt & Associates and
Center City/Inner Harbor
Development Inc., 1990

14

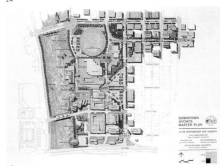

15

16

*Old San Juan Waterfront Redevelopment
San Juan, Puerto Rico
Paseo Portuario SE, a joint venture of
Rexach Construction Company and
Plaza Las Americas, 1990

Northridge at Deer Valley
Phoenix, AZ
Johnson Wax Development
Corporation, 1990

*State-Thomas Public Improvement Plan
Dallas, TX
City of Dallas, 1990

Newco Due Diligence
Kona, HI
GA Partners & Arthur Anderson, 1990

Moji Harbor Redevelopment[20]
Island of Kyushu, Japan
Seiyo•Corporation, 1990

Metairie Galleria
Metairie, LA
Westinghouse Evaluation Services
Group, 1990

MCA/Universal Studios Master Plan
Paris, France
MCA Recreation Services, 1990

Mark Center Master Plan
Alexandria, VA
The Mark Winkler Company, 1990

LBJ Corridor Study
Farmers Branch, TX
City of Farmers Branch, 1990

Knepp Castle Resort
West Sussex, England
Seibu Saison Group, 1990

Corning Visitor Center[21]
Corning, NY
Kessler Group, Inc., 1990

Church Street Station Entertainment District Expansion Master Plan
Orlando, FL
KMS Group, Inc., 1990

Chiburi Lake Golf Resort[22]
Tochigi Prefecture, Japan
Kajima Corporation, Sumitomo
Corporation, Japan View Hotel Co.,
Ltd, 1990

CenterMark
Dallas, TX
NCNB Dallas, 1990

Canmore Hyatt Resort Master Plan
Banff, Canada
Canmore Alpine Development Co., Ltd,
1990

Cameron Center Mixed-Use Master Plan
Alexandria, VA
Simpson Development Co., 1990

Allied Chemical Harborgate Site
Baltimore, MD
Allied Signal, Inc., 1990

Chicago South Loop
Chicago, IL
Walsh, Higgins & Company, 1990

Oklahoma City Arts District
Oklahoma City, OK
Oklahoma City Urban Renewal District
1991

Las Colinas Housing
Irving, TX
Las Colinas, Inc., 1991

Wisley Golf Resort
Surrey, England
HSI, Ltd, (a subsidiary of the
Seiyo•Corporation), 1991

Saku Four Season Resort Master Plan
Saku, Japan
Confidential, 1991

Old Farmers Branch Area Plan
Farmers Branch, TX
City of Farmers Branch, 1991

Via Ranch
Houston, TX
American General Investment
Corporation, 1991

17

18

19

20

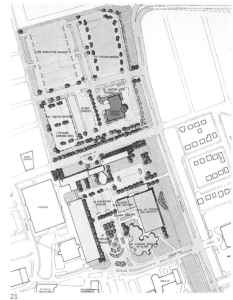

21

Nashville Center City Plan
Nashville, TN
Metropolitan Development & Housing
Agency, Metropolitan Planning
Commission, and Center City
Committee, 1991

Moreno Highlands[23]
Moreno Valley, CA
Moreno Highlands Co., 1991

**Maryland School for the Blind Campus
Utilization Master Plan**
Baltimore, MD
The Maryland School for the Blind
1991

*State-Thomas Reinvestment Zone
Dallas, TX
City of Dallas, 1991

Lyon Mixed-Use
Lyon, France
Longbow Development Company, 1991

Les Lacs Special District Plan
Addison, TX
Town of Addison, 1991

Kishiwada Port Redevelopment Plan[24]
Kishiwada City, Japan
Kishiwada Port Development Corp., 1991

Finca Monterey Master Plan
Monterey, Puerto Rico
Empresas Fonelladas, 1991

Club City Housing
Makuhari (Tokyo), Japan
Shimizu Corporation, 1991

Crescent West Mixed-Use
Dallas, TX
Rosewood Property Company, 1991

Cinco Ranch
Houston, TX
Cinco Ranch Development
Corporation, 1991

Camden Yards East
Urban Design Analysis
Baltimore, MD
The Maryland Stadium Authority, 1991

The Grand Axis at La Défense
Paris, France
L'Etablissement Public Pour
l'Aménagement de La Défense (EPAD),
1991

**Baldhead Island Resort/
Commercial Center**
Bald Head Island, SC
Baldhead Island Management Inc.
1991

Addison Comprehensive Plan[25]
Addison, TX
Town of Addison, 1991

**Abandoibarra Riverfront
Redevelopment Plan**
Bilbao, Spain
PROMOBISA, 1991

Baton Rouge Mixed-Use
Baton Rouge, LA
Royal Marque Company Ltd, 1992

Falling Waters Residential
Baton Rouge, LA
Royal Marque Company, Ltd, 1992

South Padre Barrier Island
South Padre Island, TX
American General Realty Investment
Corporation, 1992

Yeo-Su City Kyong Island Master Plan[26]
Yeo-Su City, Korea
Daewoo Corporation, 1992

NCNB/Dr Pepper Site
Dallas, TX
NCNB Dallas, 1992

**Santa Ana Pueblo Land
Development Plan**
Albuquerque, NM
Santa Ana Pueblo Tribal Council
1992

Fieldstone Farms
Franklin, TN
American General Land Development
Corp., 1992

Empire Tract
The Meadowlands, NJ
Empire Ltd, 1992

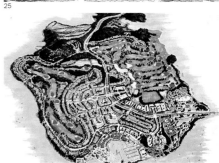

Alameda Master Plan
Mexico City, Mexico
Grupo Danhos, 1992

El Paso Renaissance
El Paso, TX
City of El Paso, 1992

Proyecto Rio Sonora
Hermosillo, Mexico
Progresso (State Development Agency)
1992

Atlantic City Gateway[27]
Atlantic City, NJ
Casino Reinvestment Development
Authority, 1993

Rangsit
Bangkok, Thailand
Central Pattana Development Co. Ltd
1994

Wanakerta Estate[28]
Jakarta, Indonesia
PT Sinar Puspapersada, 1994

Kota Indrapura Master Plan
Pekan, Kuantan, Malaysia
Malaysian Plantations Berhad, 1994

Trawas Resort Master Plan
Surabaya, Indonesia
PT Dharmala Land, 1994

Hsiao Yun International Industrial Park[29]
Weifung City, Shandong Province,
China
United International Development
Investment Inc., 1994

*Stadtquartier Lehrter Bahnhof[30]
Berlin, Germany
Tishman Speyer Properties of Berlin,
LP and Deutsche Bahn, 1994

Beijing Bakery Master Plan
Beijing, China
Sterling Enterprises, 1994

***Huangshan Furong International
Tourist Town**
Anhui Province, China
Huangshan Development Company
1995

Downtown Austin Development Plan
Austin, TX
Keyser Marston Associates Inc., 1995

Beirut Mixed-Use Master Plan
Beirut, Lebanon
The Mouawad Group, 1995

Paseo del Este
El Paso, TX
State of Texas General Land Office, 1995

Addison Circle
Addison, TX
Columbus Realty Trust, Town of
Addison, 1995

Downtown Housing District
Fort Worth, TX
Columbus Realty Trust, Sundance
Square, Inc., 1995

Lakewood Ranch
Sarasota, FL
Schroeder Manatee Ranch, Inc., 1995

Roseland Homes
Dallas, TX
Dallas Housing Authority, 1995

Richardson Comprehensive Plan Update
Richardson, TX
City of Richardson, 1995

Denton Business Parks
Denton, TX
City of Denton, Chamber of
Commerce, 1995

Concordplex
Dallas, TX
Concord Baptist Church, 1995

Deep Ellum Entertainment District[31]
Dallas, TX
Southwest Properties, 1995

Village on the Parkway
Addison, TX
Southwest Properties, 1995

Las Majadas
Guatamala City
Compania General de Urbanaciones
S.A., 1995

28

29

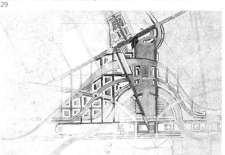
30

31

32

33

Guan Qian Jie Master Plan
  Suzhou, China
  Far East Organization, 1995

*Dalian New City Center
  Dalian, Liaoning Province, China
  Dalian Economic and Technical
  Development Zone, 1995

Cinangka Master Plan
  Bogor, Indonesia
  Bonauli Real Estate, 1995

Marina City
  East Surabaya, Indonesia
  PT Dharmala Land, 1995

Grande Family Estate
  Surabaya, Indonesia
  PT Dharmala Land, 1995

Pakuwon City Master Plan
  Tunjungan, Indonesia
  PT Pakuwon Jati, 1995

Koje-do Master Plan Study
  Korea
  Confidential, 1995

Kota Kemuning Town Centre
  Kuala Lumpur, Malaysia
  Tunas Prestasi Sdn. Bhd., 1995

Prolink 2020 Office Park[32]
  Johor, Malaysia
  Prolink Development Sdn. Bhd., 1995

Plaza Merdeka[33]
  Kuala Lumpur, Malaysia
  United Engineers (Malaysia) Bhd., 1995

Fort Bonifacio Master Plan[34]
  Makati, Metro Manila, Philippines
  Fort Bonifacio Development Corp.,
  1995

Santa Lucia Riverwalk[35]
  Monterrey, N.L., Mexico
  Consejo Estatal de Rehabilitaccion
  Urbana, 1995

China Square
  Singapore
  Far East Organization, 1995

Jurong Lake Recreational Area
  Singapore
  Singapore Technologies, 1995

Green Bay
  Taipei County, Taiwan
  Pacific Construction Co., Ltd, 1995

19 Hectare Mixed-use
  Taipei, Taiwan
  Pacific Construction Co., Ltd, 1995

Chang-Hsin Provincal Government Center
  Chang-Hsin, Taiwan
  Kaichuan Engineering Co. Ltd, 1995

Pen Chiao
  Taipei, Taiwan
  Yuan Ding Development Co., 1995

*Shae-Zee Island
  Taipei, Taiwan
  Taipei Department of City Planning
  1995

Church Street Corridor[36]
  Nashville, TN
  Nashville Metropolitan Development
  and Housing Agency, 1996

34

35

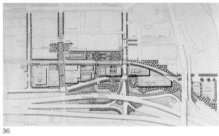

36

Awards

In addition to widespread client satisfaction with our projects, we pride ourselves on earning the recognition of our peers. Since our founding, RTKL has been the recipient of hundreds of professional society and publication-sponsored awards for architecture, engineering, planning/urban design, and graphics. RTKL, our staff, and our projects have received the following awards.

Harold L. Adams, **The Governor's Award**, The World Trade Center Institute, 1996

RTKL Washington Office, **Architectural Firm of the Year**, Metropolitan Washington Chapter of Associated Builders and Contractors, 1993

RTKL Associates Inc., **President's "E Award for Excellence in Exporting,"** US Department of Commerce, 1992

RTKL Washington Office, **Pierre L'Enfant Award for Outstanding Architect/Engineer**, Subby Awards Program, DC Metropolitan Subcontractors Association, 1990

RTKL Dallas Office, **Texas Architectural Firm of the Year Award**, Texas Construction Trade Exposition, 1987

Sub-Contractors Association of Metropolitan Baltimore Outstanding Architects, 1970

DESIGN AWARDS

Congressional Plaza, **ICSC Merit Award**, 1996

The Galleria Morley, **ICSC Merit Award**, 1996

The Entertainment Center, Irvine Spectrum, **SADI Award**, 1996

The Galleria Morley, **SADI Award**, 1996

Health Care Financing Administration Headquarters, **Craftsmanship Award**, Washington Building Congress, 1996

Reston Town Center Pavilion, **Merit Award**, Washington Chapter/AIA, 1995

Architecture and Planning/Urban Design Brandon Town Center, **Merit Award**, Metal Construction Association, 1995

Harbor View Townhomes, Mud Island, **Aurora Award**, (Attached For-Sale Homes, $150,000–$200,000), 1995

The Galleria Morley, **Gold Nugget Grand Award** (Commercial Retail Category), Pacific Coast Builders Conference, 1995

Kota Indrapura, **Gold Nugget Merit Award**, Pacific Coast Builders Conference, 1995

Shae-Zee Island Masterplan, **Gold Nugget Merit Award**, Pacific Coast Builders Conference, 1995

Plaza San Augustine, **Merit Award**, Dallas Chapter/AIA, 1995

Reston Town Center Pavilion, **Merit Award**, Washington Chapter/AIA, 1995

First Union Center, **Building of the Year** (100,000–249,900-SF Category), Southern Region, BOMA, 1995

Reston Town Center Pavilion, **Design Award**, Baltimore Chapter/AIA, 1994

Club Industrial de Monterey, **Unbuilt Award**, Dallas Chapter/AIA, 1994

National Maritime Intelligence Center, **Department of Defense Design Excellence**, Administrative Facilities, 1994

National Maritime Intelligence Center, **Craftsmanship Award**, Washington Building Congress, 1994

Harbor View Townhomes, Mud Island, **Grand Award**, Best in American Living Awards, 1994

Oriole Park at Camden Yards, **Public Award**, ULI Award for Excellence, 1994

Shae-Zee Island Development Plan, **Merit Award**, Boston Society of Landscape Architects, 1994

Valencia Town Center, **Design Award**, Innovative Design and Construction, International Council of Shopping Centers, 1994

Roosevelt Field, **Design Award**, International Council of Shopping Centers, 1994

The Boulevard, **Merit Award**, International Council of Shopping Centers, 1994

Willowbrook Mall, **Merit Award**, International Council of Shopping Centers, 1994

Francis Scott Key Pavilion at Johns Hopkins Bayview Medical Center, **Honorable Mention**, Baltimore Chapter/AIA, 1994

Francis Scott Key Pavilion at Johns Hopkins Bayview Medical Center, **Merit Award**, Maryland Society/AIA, 1994

Bancroft Hall Phase I Renovation, US Naval Academy, **Excellent Performance Evaluation**, Naval Facilities Engineering Command (NAVFAC)/Chesapeake Division, 1994

Bancroft Hall Masterplan, US Naval Academy, **Certification of Appreciation in Recognition of Exemplary Performance**, Naval Facilities Engineering Command (NAVFAC)/Chesapeake Division, 1993

Christiana Mall, **Winner, Retail, Building Excellence Awards of the Delaware Valley**, 1993

525 B Street, **Design Award**, Rehabilitated/Modernized Building, Los Angeles Chapter/BOMA, 1993

Harold L. Adams, **Gold Medal** by Tau Sigma Delta, the National Honor Society for Architecture and The Allied Arts, 1993

Boulevard Mall, **Citation**, Dallas Chapter/AIA, 1993

Menlo Park, **Design Award**, International Council of Shopping Centers, 1993

Fairfax County Government Center, **Honor Award**, Fairfax County Exceptional Design Awards Program, 1993

Greater Baltimore Medical Center Obstetrics/Acute Care Expansion, **Design Award**, Baltimore Chapter/AIA, 1993

Greater Baltimore Medical Center Obstetrics/Acute Care Expansion, **Outstanding Project Award**, New Projects over $10 million, Baltimore Metropolitan Chapter/Associated Builders and Contractors, Inc., 1993

The Ryland Group Inc. Headquarters, **Honorable Mention**, New Projects over $10 million, Baltimore Metropolitan Chapter/Associated Builders and Contractors, Inc., 1993

Boulevard Mall, **Co-Winner**, Renovated Enclosed Mall over 500,000 SF, *Monitor* Centers and Stores of Excellence, 1993

Valencia Town Center, **Honorable Mention**, New Enclosed Mall over 500,000 SF, *Monitor* Centers and Stores of Excellence, 1993

Garden Food Court at Cumberland Mall, **Honorable Mention**, Renovated Enclosed Mall under 500,000 SF, *Monitor* Centers and Stores of Excellence, 1993

A&S Roosevelt Field, **Honorable Mention**, Full-Line Department Store, *Monitor* Centers and Stores of Excellence, 1993

Reston Town Center, One and Two Fountain Square, **Best of Virginia Award**, Office Buildings over 20,000 SF, Associated General Contractors of Virginia, 1993

Reston Town Center, **AIA Urban Design Award of Excellence**, 1992

The Camden Yards Sports Complex Development Plan (master plan and urban design for Oriole Park), **AIA Urban Design Award of Excellence**, 1992

Tysons Corner Center, **Urban Land Institute Award for Excellence**, Rehabilitation Category, 1992

Fieldstone Farms Residential Master Plan, **Greater Nashville Regional Council Award for Excellence in Development**, 1992

British Aerospace Customer Support Facility, **Merit Award**, Best Corporate Build-to-Suit, Northern Virginia Chapter/NAIOP, 1992

British Aerospace Customer Support Facility, **Merit Award**, Best Master Plan, Northern Virginia Chapter/NAIOP, 1992

British Aerospace Customer Support Facility, **Merit Award**, Best Mixed-Use Facility, Northern Virginia Chapter/NAIOP, 1992

The Manhattan, **Grand Award**, Hotel Category, Gold Nugget Awards (Pacific Coast Builders Conference and *Sun/Coast Architect/Builder* magazine, 1992

The Camden Yards Sports Complex Development Plan (master plan and urban design for Oriole Park), **Honor Award**, Design Category, ASLA Professional Awards, 1992

The Camden Yards Sports Complex Development Plan (master plan and urban design for Oriole Park), **Merit Award**, Planning and Urban Design Category, ASLA Professional Awards, 1992

Montgomery Mall, **Grand Award**, Interior Landscape Installation above $50,000, MD/DC/VA Landscape Contractors Association, 1992

Bank One Center, **Outstanding Contribution to the Revitalization of Cleveland**, Greater Cleveland Growth Association's Downtown Business Council, 1992

525 B Street, **Downtown Improvement Award**, Central City Association, 1992

Menlo Park, **Co-Winner**, New Enclosed Mall over 500,000 SF, *Monitor* Centers and Stores of Excellence, 1992

Towson Town Center, **Honorable Mention**, New Enclosed Mall over 500,000 SF, *Monitor* Centers and Stores of Excellence, 1992

Reston Town Center, **Grand Award**, Best Commercial Project over 150,000-SF, National Association of Home Builders' National Commercial Builders Council, 1992

Reston Town Center, **First Place**, Commercial over $25 million, Excellence in Construction Awards, Associated Builders and Contractors, 1992

Reston Town Center, **Award for Design Excellence**, Architectural Precast Association, 1992

Boulevard Cafés at Montgomery Mall, **Best Interior Retail/Restaurant Space**, Washington/Suburban Maryland Chapter/NAIOP, 1992

Democracy Plaza, **Best Mixed-Use Park**, Washington/Suburban Maryland Chapter/NAIOP, 1992

Democracy Plaza II Office Building, **Best Suburban Office Building Over 150,000 SF**, Washington/Suburban Maryland Chapter/NAIOP, 1992

Menlo Park, **First Place Winner**, Marble Category, Ninth Annual Masonry Awards Program, New Jersey State Conference of Bricklayers & Allied Craftsmen/Mason Contractors of New Jersey, 1992

Bay Plaza South Core Retail/Parking Complex, **Peer Jury Award of Merit**, Tampa Bay Chapter/AIA, 1992

Sculpture Studio, **AIA Honor Award**, 1991

Sculpture Studio, **American School and University Architectural Portfolio**, 1991

Courtyard Shops of Encino, **Valley Development Breakfast Club's First Annual "Flash" Award**, 1991

Courtyard Shops of Encino, **Athena Award**, Best New Commercial Project, Encino Chamber of Commerce, 1991

IBM Information Systems Services Data Processing Center, The Builders Exchange of Rochester, Inc., **Craftsmanship Award**, 1991

First Union Bank Building, **Award Winner**, Broward Builders Exchange, Inc., Granite & Marble Installation, Granite/Exterior Cladding, Elevator Installation Foreman, 1991

Reston Town Center, **Excellence in Architecture**, Iron Workers Employers Association (IWEA), 1991

Concord Street Substation, **First Prize, Environmental Aesthetics; Third Prize, Systems**, *Electrical World* magazine, 1991

The Camden Yards Sports Complex Development Plan (master plan and urban design for Oriole Park), **Grand Design Award**, Baltimore Chapter/AIA, 1991

The Fashion Centre at Pentagon City, **Urban Land Institute Award for Excellence**, Large-Scale, Urban Mixed-Use Development Category, 1991

Marsh & McLennan Building, **Honor Award**, Maryland Society of Architects, 1991

Marsh & McLennan Building, **Historic Preservation Project Award**, Maryland Historical Trust, 1991

Reston Town Center, **Citation**, Maryland Society of Architects, 1991

Reston Town Center, **Award of Excellence**, Best Master Plan, Northern Virginia Chapter/NAIOP, 1991

Reston Town Center, **Award of Excellence**, Best Community Strip Center, Northern Virginia Chapter/NAIOP, 1991

Reston Town Center, **Award of Excellence**, Best Hotel/Mixed-Use Facilities, Virginia Chapter/NAIOP, 1991

Reston Town Center, **Award of Excellence**, Best People/Public Spaces, Northern Virginia/NAIOP, 1991

Reston Town Center, Best Mixed-Use Project over 200,000 SF, **Cornerstone Award**, DC/NoVa/Suburban MD Building Industry Association, 1991

Reston Town Center Fountain Square, **Honor Award**, Northern Virginia Community Appearance Alliance, 1991

Reston Town Center, **Award of Excellence**, Commercial Projects over $40 million, Washington Metropolitan and Virginia Chapters/ Associated Builders and Contractors, 1991

Tower City Center, **First Award**, Downtown Development Award, Downtown Research and Development Center, 1991

The Avenue at Tower City Center, **First Place, Adaptive Use, Renovation Design Awards**, *Commercial Renovation*, 1991

The Avenue at Tower City Center, **Design Award**, International Council of Shopping Centers, 1991

The Avenue at Tower City Center, **Co-Winner**, Adaptive Reuse, *Monitor* Centers and Stores of Excellence, 1991

The Avenue at Tower City Center, **Superior Achievement in Design and Imaging (SADI) Award**, Renovated Enclosed Center, 1991

Tiffany & Co., **Building Excellence Award of the Delaware Valley**, 1991

Downtown Raleigh Plan, **Outstanding Planning Implementation Award**, Maryland Chapter/APA, 1991

Downtown Raleigh Plan, **Merit Award**, International Downtown Association, 1991

Harbor Town, **Merit Award**, Landscape/Urban Design, Maryland Chapter/ASLA, 1991

Harbor Town, **Merit Award**, Builder's Choice Design and Planning Awards, 1991

Harbor Town, **Planning Award of Excellence**, Tennessee Chapter/American Planning Association, 1991

Shin Shirakawa Resort Hotel and Golf Clubhouse, **Design Award**, Baltimore Chapter/AIA, 1991

Cumberland Mall, **Certificate of Merit**, International Council of Shopping Centers, 1991

Cumberland Mall, **Co-Winner**, Renovated Enclosed Mall over 1 million SF, *Monitor* Centers and Stores of Excellence, 1991

Hamilton Eaton Centre, **Co-Winner**, New Enclosed Mall under 500,000 SF, *Monitor* Centers and Stores of Excellence, 1991

Democracy Plaza, **Merit Award**, Commercial over 150,000 SF, National Commercial Builders Council of National Association of Home Builders, 1991

Hyatt Charlotte, **Gold Key Award**, Excellence in Lobby Design, American Hotel & Motel Association and *Designer Specifier*, 1990

The Fashion Centre at Pentagon City, **Certificate of Merit**, International Council of Shopping Centers, 1990

Marsh & McLennan Building, **Grand Design Award**, Baltimore Chapter/AIA, 1990

Marsh & McLennan Building, **Craftsmanship Award**, Building Congress and Exchange of Metropolitan Baltimore, 1990

Marsh & McLennan Building, **Outstanding Project Award**, Baltimore Metropolitan Chapter/Associated Builders and Contractors, 1990

Marsh & McLennan Building, **Preservation Building Award**, Baltimore Heritage, 1990

Marsh & McLennan Building, **Amarlite Architectural Products Environmental Award**, Curtainwall, 1990

Sculpture Studio, **Design Award**, Baltimore Chapter/AIA, 1990

Pentagon City, Outstanding Achievement in a Mixed-Use Project over 200,000 SF, **Cornerstone Award**, DC/NoVa/Suburban MD Building Industry Association, 1990

A&S Plaza, **Second Place**, Store Facade/Exterior Design, Worldstore '90 International Store Design Competition, 1990

Reston Town Center, One Fountain Square, **First Place**, Best Office Building over 150,000 SF, Northern Virginia/NAIOP, 1990

Tysons Corner Center, **Modernization Award of Excellence**, Buildings, 1990

Tysons Corner Center, Fairfax County (VA) **Exceptional Design Award**, 1990

University of Maryland at Baltimore Dental School, **finalist**, corporate/single user, BOMA/Metropolitan Baltimore, 1990

University of Maryland Medical System, **Associate AIA Award**, Baltimore Chapter/AIA, 1990

Esperanté, **Award of Excellence**, Broward County/AIA, 1990

State-Thomas Area Plan, **Award of Merit**, Dallas Chapter/AIA, 1990

Coliseum Mall, **Co-Winner**, *Monitor* Centers and Stores of Excellence, 1990

Erin Mills Town Centre, **Honorable Mention**, *Monitor* Centers and Stores of Excellence, 1990

The Fashion Mall at Plantation, **Honorable Mention**, *Monitor* Centers and Stores of Excellence, 1990

The Bellevue, **Honorable Mention**, *Monitor* Centers and Stores of Excellence, 1990

Pavilion Saks Fifth Avenue, **Honorable Mention**, *Monitor* Centers and Stores of Excellence, 1990

Burdines at The Gardens, **Best of Show**, Night Beautiful, 1990

Burdines at The Gardens, **New Store of the Year Award**, *Chain Store Age Executive*, 1990

Reston Town Center, **Craftsmanship Award**, Washington (DC) Building Congress, 1990

The Fashion Centre at Pentagon City, **Craftsmanship Award**, Washington (DC) Building Congress, 1990

Neiman Marcus at Tysons II, **Craftsmanship Award**, Washington (DC) Building Congress, 1990

Tysons Corner Center, **Craftsmanship Award**, Washington (DC) Building Congress, 1990

Washington Center, **Merit Shop Construction Award**, Commercial, over $20 million, Metropolitan Washington and Virginia Chapters/Associated Builders and Contractors, 1990

Washington Center, **NAIOP Excellence in Design & Development**, Office Buildings over 200,000 SF, 1990

Washington Center, **Craftsmanship Award**, Washington (DC) Building Congress, 1990

901 E Street, **Craftsmanship Award**, Washington (DC) Building Congress, 1990

Fashion Mall at Keystone at the Crossing, **Merit Award**, Urban Design Section of the Indianapolis Department of Metropolitan Development, 1990

Costa do Sol, **Unbuilt Design Award**, Florida Association of Architects, 1990

Bay Plaza Waterfront Retail District, **Unbuilt Design Award**, Florida Association of Architects, 1990

A&S Plaza, **Modernization and Restoration Award**, New York Chapter/BOMA, 1990

Manhattan Town Center, **Honorable Mention**, *Monitor* Centers and Stores of Excellence, 1989

Burdines at The Gardens, **Co-Winner**, *Monitor* Centers and Stores of Excellence, 1989

Strawbridge & Clothier at King of Prussia Mall, **Luxury Department Store of the Year**, Chain Store Age Executive, 1989

Tysons Corner Center, **Design Award**, International Council of Shopping Centers, 1989

Tysons Corner Center, **Design Award**, *Monitor* Centers and Stores of Excellence, 1989

Esperanté, **Design '89 Honor Award**, National Association of Industrial and Office Parks, 1989

Bay Plaza Waterfront Retail District, **Unbuilt Design Award**, Broward County/AIA, 1989

Palmer Square North, **Merit Award**, Annual Concrete Award, New Jersey Concrete and Aggregate Association and American Concrete Institute/New Jersey Chapter, 1989

Harbor Town, Mud Island, **Downtown (Memphis) Award for Housing and Neighborhood Development**, 1989

Hyatt Plaza in Fair Lakes, **Award of Excellence**, Best Office Building over 150,000 SF, Northern Virginia/NAIOP, 1989

Fairview Park, **Design Award**, Northern Virginia Community Appearance Alliance, 1988

Building 111, Washington Navy Yard, **Excellence in Design for Improvement Projects**, US Department of Defense Design Awards for Excellence, 1988

Building 111, Washington Navy Yard, Outstanding, Restoration/Renovation over $1 million, **Merit Shop Construction Award**, VA/Metropolitan DC/Associated Builders and Contractors, 1988

Manhattan Town Center, **Award of Design Excellence**, Broward County Chapter/AIA, 1988

Tysons Corner Center Parking Terraces, **Honorable Mention**, Precast Concrete Institute, 1988

Pavilion Saks Fifth Avenue, **Certificate of Merit**, International Council of Shopping Centers, 1988

Bay Plaza Waterfront Retail District, **Design Award of Excellence**, Broward County Chapter/AIA, 1988

Bay Plaza Waterfront Retail District, **Design Award of Excellence**, Florida Association of Architects, 1988

AT&T Customer Technology Center, **Co-Winner**, *Monitor* Centers and Stores of Excellence, 1988

Burdines at The Gardens, **Co-Winner**, *Monitor* Centers and Stores of Excellence, 1988

Strawbridge & Clothier at King of Prussia Mall, **Co-Winner**, *Monitor* Centers and Stores of Excellence, 1988

Computer Sciences Corporation Regional Headquarters, **Design Award**, NAIOP, 1988

Harbor Town, Mud Island, **Design Award**, Baltimore Chapter/AIA, 1988

Manhattan Town Center, **National Council for Urban Economic Development Award**, 1988

Manhattan Town Center, **Design Award**, Broward County Chapter/AIA, 1988

Village at Shirlington, **Modernization Award**, *Buildings*, 1988

Town Center at Cobb, **Honorable Mention**, *Monitor* Centers and Stores of Excellence, 1988

Gwinnett Place Phase II Expansion, **Honorable Mention**, *Monitor* Centers and Stores of Excellence, 1988

Sumner School, **Preservation Award**, Washington Chapter/AIA, 1987

State-Thomas Plan, **Community Honor Award**, Dallas Chapter/AIA, 1987

Eton Square, **NCMA Concrete Paver Award of Excellence**, 1987

Owings Mills Town Center, **Award of Excellence**, American Institute of Steel Construction, 1987

Central Park at Mid Cities, **Annual Award**, American Planning Association, 1987

Richardson Plan, **Merit Award**, American Planning Association, 1987

Galleria at South Bay, **Honorable Mention**, *National Mall Monitor* Design Award, 1987

Town Center at Boca, **Honorable Mention**, *National Mall Monitor* Design Award, 1987

Ballston Common, **Co-Winner**, *National Mall Monitor* Design Award, 1987

St Louis Centre, **Co-Winner**, *National Mall Monitor* Design Award, 1987

Town Center at Boca Expansion, **Design Award**, International Council of Shopping Centers, 1987

Galleria at South Bay, **Design Award**, International Council of Shopping Centers, 1987

One City Centre, **Award**, National Association of Industrial and Office Parks, 1987

Central Park at Mid-Cities, **Award**, National Association of Industrial and Office Parks, 1987

Eton Square, **Award**, National Association of Industrial and Office Parks, 1987

Polo Park, **Design Award**, International Council of Shopping Centers, 1987

The Promenade, **Design Award**, International Council of Shopping Centers, 1987

Sumner Square and School Renovation, **Citation**, Mayor's Architectural Design Awards, 1986

Plaza Shops at Crystal City, Renovation, **Cornerstone Award**, 1986

IBM Education Center at Thornwood, **Design Award**, Baltimore Chapter/AIA, 1986

St Louis Centre, **Achievement Award**, International Downtown Association, 1986

Bank of Baltimore Interiors, **Honor Award**, Baltimore Chapter/AIA, 1986

Church of the Redeemer, **25-Year Award**, Baltimore Chapter/AIA, 1986

USF+G Mount Washington Center, **Creative Adaptive Re-Use Award**, National Association of Industrial and Office Parks, Maryland/Washington Chapter, 1985

Signet Tower, **High-rise Office Award**, National Association of Industrial and Office Parks, Maryland/Washington Chapter, 1985

Charles Center Metro Station, **Excellence in Concrete Award**, American Concrete Institute, Maryland Chapter, 1985

Charles Center Metro Station, **Honor Award**, Baltimore Chapter/AIA, 1985

Charleston Town Center, **Award of Excellence**, *National Mall Monitor*, 1985

Inner Harbor Center, **Honor Award**, Baltimore Chapter/AIA, 1982

Tower City Terminal Concourses, **Certificate of Exceptional Accomplishment for Preservation, Restoration, and Adaptive Use**, Cleveland Chapter/AIA, 1982

Town Center at Boca, **Honor Award**, Baltimore Chapter/AIA, 1982

Impact Dallas Competition, **Honor Award**, Dallas Chapter/AIA, 1981

Willow Grove Park, **Master Builder in Steel Award**, Mid-Atlantic Steel Fabricators Association, 1981

Suburban Square, **Honor Award**, American Society of Landscape Architects/Maryland Chapter, 1981

Suburban Square, **Honor Award**, Baltimore Chapter/AIA, 1981

The Federated Building, **Honor Award**, Baltimore Chapter/AIA, 1981

Beachwood Mall, **Honor Award**, Baltimore Chapter/AIA, 1981

Plan for Downtown Clearwater, **Merit Award**, American Planning Association/Florida Chapter, 1980

Cincinnati Skywalk System, **Downtown Achievement Award**, International Downtown Executives Association, 1979

Johns Hopkins Medical Institutions, **State of Maryland Award of Merit for Barrier-Free Design**, 1978

Johns Hopkins Medical Institutions, **Honor Award**, Maryland Society of Architects, 1978

Corning City Hall and Public Library, **Honor Award**, Maryland Society of Architects, 1978

Joseph H. Rash Memorial Park, **Environmental Improvement National Grand Award**, Associated Landscape Contractors of America, 1978

Joseph H. Rash Memorial Park, **American Society of Landscape Architects Merit Award**, 1977

Corning Public Library, **AIA-ALA Library Buildings Award Program Award of Merit**, 1976

Southwestern High School, **Award of Merit**, Baltimore Chapter/AIA, 1975

West 20 Housing for the Elderly, **Honor Award**, Baltimore Chapter/AIA, 1975

University of Maryland Baltimore County Campus Library, **Honor Award**, Baltimore Chapter/AIA, 1975

Cincinnati CBD & Fountain Square, **AIA Citation for Excellence in Community Architecture**, 1974

Southern Ohio Bank, **Award of Excellence for Design/Interiors**, Architectural Record, 1974

Paramus Park Shopping Center, **Architectural Award of Excellence**, American Institute of Steel Construction, 1974

Fountain Square, **AIA Honor Award**, 1973

Calvert County Vocational Technical Training Center, **Award of Excellence**, American Institute of Steel Construction, 1972

GSA Bioscience Laboratory, **Merit Award**, GSA First Biennial Design Award Program, 1972

South County Library, **AIA-ALA Library Buildings Award Program Award of Merit**, 1972

St Timothy's Performing Arts Center, **Honor Award**, Baltimore Chapter/AIA, 1972

GSA Bioscience Laboratory, **Award**, Potomac Valley Chapter/AIA, 1972

Albany Riverfront Pumping Station, **New York State Council of the Arts Award**, 1971

Charles Plaza, Charles Center, **Honor Award**, Department of Housing and Urban Development, 1970

Hopkins Plaza, Charles Center, **Certificate of Merit**, American Association of Nurserymen Landscape Award, 1970

Albany Riverfront Pumping Station, **Certificate of Merit**, New York State Society of Architects, 1970

Two Charles Center, **First Honor Award**, Baltimore Region/AIA, 1969

Charles Plaza, **Honor Award**, Middle Atlantic Region/AIA, 1969

Montgomery Village, Court Garden Houses, **Design Award**, AIA House and Home Steel Institute, 1968

Montgomery Village, Court Garden Houses, **Honor Award**, Potomac Valley Chapter/AIA, 1968

Charles Center Office Building Design Competition, Baltimore Area 16B Office Tower, 1968

John Deere Branch House, **AIA Honor Award**, 1968

John Deere Branch House, **Award of Honor**, Chamber of Commerce of Metropolitan Baltimore, 1968

John Deere Branch House, **Design in Steel Award**, American Iron and Steel Institute, 1967

Greater Baltimore Medical Center, **Medical Facilities Modern Hospital of the Month**, 1966

The Charles Center Project, **Award of Merit**, Housing and Home Finance Agency, 1964

Church of the Redeemer, **AIA Award of Merit**, 1958

Annapolis Girl Scout Lodge, **AIA Award of Merit**, 1954

Harundale Mall Shopping Center, **Award of Merit**, National Institute of Home Builders, 1952

INTERIOR ARCHITECTURE AND DESIGN

RTKL Washington Office, **Craftsmanship Award**, Architectural Millwork, Washington Building Congress, 1995

Coopers & Lybrand, **Craftsmanship Award**, Finishes, Plaster, and Drywall, Washington Building Congress, 1995

201 East Pine Street Lobby, **Golden Brick Award**, Interior Design, Downtown Orlando Partnership, 1995

Legg Mason Wood Walker, Inc., **Special Recognition Award**, Creative Millwork Detailing, Institute of Business Designers (IBD)/Potomac Chapter, 1994

Fairfax County Government Center, **Outstanding Achievement Award**, Institute of Business Designers (IBD)/Potomac Chapter, 1993

Whiting-Turner Contracting Company, **Outstanding Achievement Award**, Institute of Business Designers (IBD)/Potomac Chapter and Regardie's, 1992

Bank of Baltimore Executive Offices, **Outstanding Achievement Award**, Institute of Business Designers (IBD)/Potomac Chapter and Regardie's, 1990

Catholic Relief Services, **Special Recognition Award for Creative Use of Existing Building Structure**, (IBD)/Potomac Chapter and Regardie's, 1990

Baltimore Visitors Center, **Special Recognition Award for Creative Use of Signage and Graphics**, (IBD)/Potomac Chapter and Regardie's, 1990

Princeton Marriott Forrestal Village, **Best Hotel over 300 Rooms**, *Restaurant/Hotel Design International*, 1988

Bank of Baltimore Executive Offices, **Honor Award for Design Excellence**, Baltimore Chapter/AIA, 1986

ENGINEERING

Commerce Place, Class A Office Tower, **First Place**, ASHRAE Region III Technology Award, 1995

Health Care Financing Administration Headquarters, **Craftsmanship Award**, Installation and Fabrication of Electrical Work, Building Congress & Exchange, 1995

Chicago O'Hare Airport, elevated track structure for automated guideway transit system, **Most Innovative Structure Award**, Structural Engineers Association of Illinois, 1993

1830 East Monument Street, New Commercial Buildings, **First Place**, ASHRAE Region III, 1991

Redwood Tower, **First Place**, ASHRAE Region III Award, 1990

One Democracy Plaza, **Second Place**, ASHRAE Region III Award, 1990

Tysons Corner Center Parking Garages, **Award**, Precast Concrete Institute, 1989

Hartford Hospital Medical Office Building, **Second Place**, ASHRAE Region III Award, 1988

Eton Square, **NCMA Concrete Paver Award of Excellence**, 1987

Owings Mills Town Center, **Award of Excellence**, American Institute of Steel Construction, 1987

IBM Education Center at Thornwood, New Commercial Building, **ASHRAE Region III Award**, 1987

Northpark Mall, **ASHRAE Region III Award**, 1986

First City Center, **Illuminating Design Award**, Illuminating Engineers Society, 1985

Valley View Mall, **Illuminating Design Award**, Illuminating Engineers Society, 1985

Inner Harbor Center, **ASHRAE Region III Award**, 1984

White Marsh Mall, **Award of Excellence**, American Institute of Steel Construction, 1983

The Federated Building, **Award of Excellence**, American Institute of Steel Construction, 1979

IBM Manufacturing Facility, **Honor Award**, Consulting Engineers Council USA, 1973

GRAPHICS

Congressional Plaza, **ICSC Merit Award**, 1996

The Entertainment Center at Irvine Spectrum, **SADI Award**, 1996

Canal Walk Cafes at Georgetown Park, **First Place**, *Signs of the Times*, 1995

Valencia Town Center, **Design Award, Innovative Design and Construction**, ICSC, 1994

The Boulevard, **Merit Award**, ICSC, 1994

RTKL Christmas Cards, **Honorable Mention**, SMPS, 1993

RTKL Special Retail and Government Brochures, **Honorable Mention**, SMPS, 1993

Boulevard Mall, **Certificate of Excellence**, Dallas Society of Visual Communications, 1993

Boulevard Mall and Panorama Cafes, **DESI Award of Excellence**, *Graphic Design:USA*, 1993

Boulevard Cafes at Montgomery Mall, **Best Interior Retail/Restaurant Space**, Washington/Suburban Maryland Chapter/NAIOP, 1992

Towson Town Center, **AIGA 50 Design Competition**, AIGA DC Chapter, 1992

Reston Town Center, **AIGA 50 Design Competition**, DC Chapter/American Institute of Graphic Designers, 1992

RTKL Newsletter, **Gold Award** (Best Special or Single Issue Design, Corporate), Ozzie Award for Design Excellence, Magazine Design & Production, 1992

RTKL Newsletters, **First State Award**, International Association of Business Communicators/Delaware Chapter, 1992

RTKL Newsletter, **Honorable Mention** (Best Overall Design, Newsletter), Ozzie Award for Design Excellence, Magazine Design and Production, 1991

Reston Town Center, **Silver Design Award**, Society of Environmental Graphic Designers, 1991

Lackawanna Station, **Certificate of Merit**, International Council of Shopping Centers, 1991

A&S Plaza, **Honorable Mention**, Society of Environmental Graphic Designers, 1990

A&S Plaza, **Second Place**, Store Facade/Exterior Design, Worldstore '90 International Store Design Competition, 1990

The Fashion Center at Pentagon City, **Certificate of Merit**, ICSC, 1990

Tower City's Steam Diner food court logo, **Art Direction Creativity '90 traveling show and Annual**, 1990

RTKL Newsletters, **First Place Award**, SMPS, 1990

Context/Environmental Graphics, **Art Direction Creativity '90 traveling show and Annual**, 1990

Context/Environmental Graphics, **Best of Show**, SMPS, 1990

Context/Environmental Graphics, **First Place Award**, SMPS, 1990

Context/Environmental Graphics, **Bronze Award** (Best Special or Single Issue Design, Corporate), Ozzie Award for Design Excellence, Magazine Design and Production, 1990

1989 RTKL Holiday Card, **HOW Self-Promotion**, 1990

Context/Planning and Urban Design, **Bronze Award** (Best Special or Single Issue Design, Corporate), Ozzie Award for Design Excellence, Magazine Design and Production, 1989

RTKL Newsletters, **First Place Award**, SMPS, 1989

RTKL Traveling Exhibition, **Honorable Mention**, SMPS, 1989

Collin Creek Mall environmental graphics, **Second Place**, *Signs of the Times*, 1989

RTKL Recruiting Brochure, **Print Regional Design Annual**, 1988

RTKL Firm Brochure, **Honorable Mention**, SMPS, 1987

Owings Mills Town Center, **Award of Excellence**, SEGD, 1987

Owings Mills Town Center, **Print Award**, SEGD, 1987

St Louis Centre, **Print Awards**, SEGD, 1987

Town Center at Boca, **Honorable Mention**, *National Mall Monitor* Design Awards, 1987

Woodbine Centre, **Honor Award**, SEGD, 1987

The Esplanade, **Merit Award**, SEGD, 1987

RTKL Recruiting Newsletter, Special Market Brochure, **First Place Award**, SMPS, 1987

RTKL Newsletters, **Second Place Award**, SMPS, 1987

Trade Show Program, **First Place Award**, SMPS, 1987

The George Washington University Center Brochure, Special Market Brochure, **Third Place Award**, SMPS, 1987

Recruiting Brochure, **Award**, Print Magazine, 1986

St Louis Centre, **Achievement Award**, International Downtown Association, 1986

RTKL Newsletter, **First Place Award**, SMPS, 1985

USF+G Mount Washington Campus, **Best in Environmental Graphics**, Print Casebook, 1985

Dallas Anniversary Poster, **Regional Design Annual**, Print Magazine, 1985

White Marsh Mall, **Best in Environmental Graphics**, Print Casebook, 1984

Mazza Gallerie, **Best in Environmental Graphics**, Print Casebook, 1984

RTKL Newsletter, **First Place Award**, SMPS, 1983

Town Center at Boca Raton, **Best in Environmental Graphics**, Print Casebook, 1982

RTKL Newsletter, **First Place Award**, SMPS, 1982

Art Directors Club of Metropolitan Washington, **Thirty-Third Annual Exhibition**, 1982

Art Directors Club of Metropolitan Washington, **Thirty-Second Annual Exhibition**, 1981

RTKL Newsletter, **First Place Award**, SMPS, 1981

Direct Mail Piece, **First Place Award**, SMPS, 1980

Bibliography

RTKL Selected Periodicals Bibliography

Baker, James R. "Bank One and interiors of the 1990's." *Texas Architect* (November–December 1991): vol. 41, no. 6, pp. 17–19.

Barna, Joel Warren. "38th Annual TSA Design Awards." *Texas Architect* (November–December 1992): vol. 42, no. 6, pp. 35–63.

Barna, Joel Warren. "Cleveland recentered [Tower City Center]." *Texas Architect* (September–October 1992): vol. 42, no. 5, pp. 56–59.

Barna, Joel Warren. "Export architecture." *Texas Architect* (November–December 1990): vol. 40, no. 6, pp. 43–52.

Barna, Joel Warren. "Working workplaces: five architects' offices." *Texas Architect* (January–February 1988): vol. 38, no.1, pp. 19–21.

Barna, Joel Warren. "AT&T's Dallas techno palace." *Texas Architect* (July–August 1988): vol. 38, no. 4, pp. 36–37.

Birney, Dion. "Hail Britannia [Hyatt Regency Grand Cayman, Grand Cayman, British West Indies]." *Restaurant/Hotel Design International* (June 1988): vol. 10, no. 6, pp. 80–85.

Brotman, David J. "DongAn Market: a historic open-air market embraces the 21st century." *Urban Land* (September 1994): vol. 53, no. 9, pp. 9–10.

Bruno, Juliet. "Concrete in a classical context: Esperante, West Palm Beach, Florida." *Florida Architect* (September–October 1990): vol. 37, no. 5, pp. 22–24.

"Buildings in the news." *Architectural Record* (March 1978): vol. 163, no. 3, pp. 40–41.

"Building Types Study 522: International resorts, overseas designs by American architects." *Architectural Record* (September 1978): vol. 164, no. 4, pp. [129]–144.

Carr, F. Housley. "Attention to Detailer Keeps Job's Team Cool [Health Care Financing Administration Headquarters]," *ENR* (July 18, 1994): p. 18.

Capuano, Alessandra. "Sul fronte del porto." *Controspazio* (July–September 1985): vol. 16, no. 3, pp. 30–[57].

"Centro: ein Freizeit und Einkaufspark in Oberhausen." *Architektur, Innenarchitektur, Technischer Ausbau* (September 1994): vol. 102, no. 9, p. 23.

Chalmers, Ray. "Mall inspires urban renaissance." *Building Design & Construction* (October 1984): vol. 25, no. 10, pp. 56–59.

Cox, Rachel. "Capitol gains: raising recognition of D.C.'s black landmarks." *Preservation News* (September 1987): vol. 27, no. 9, pp. 6, 21.

"Crossroads of San Antonio, San Antonio, Texas." *Urban Land Institute. Project Reference File* (January–March 1994): vol. 24, no. 4, pp. [1–4].

Dana, Amy. "Artistic activity." *Interiors* (July 1990): vol. 149, no. 12, pp. 80–81.

Davidsen, Judith. "Inner glow: Menlo Park Mall; Edison, New Jersey; RTKL Associates, Architect; T. Kondos Associates, Inc., Lighting Designers." *Architectural Record* (February 1993): vol. 181, no. 2 (suppl.), pp. [30]–[33].

Dean, Andrea Oppenheimer. "New town downtown: Reston Town Center, Reston, Virginia: RTKL Associates." *Architecture* (December 1991): vol. 80, no. 12, pp. 56–61.

DeMarco, Anthony DeMarco. "A Government Center By the People, For the People." *Facilities Design & Management* (January 1996): vol. 15, no.1, pp. 26–31.

"Development economics in-town planning 2: six case studies." *Architects' Journal* (May 25, 1988): vol. 187, no. 21, pp. 59–65, 67–69.

Doyle, Margaret. "Complex structural system supports Baltimore tower." *Building Design & Construction* (January 1988): vol. 29, no. 1, pp. 52–57.

"Eton Square." *Texas Architect* (November–December 1986): vol. 36, no. 6, pp. 70–71.

Fernberg, Patricia M. "Excellence in Facility Management: Practice Makes Perfect Office," *Managing Office Technology*, (December 1995): vol. 40, no. 12, pp. 14–16.

"Focus on preservation." *Architectural Record* (March 1991): vol. 179, no. 3, pp. 152–155.

Forsyth, Mark. "Mall makeovers." *Texas Architect* (July–August 1995): vol. 45, no. 4, pp. 38–41.

Franks, Julia. "Special addition [Radisson Suite Hotel, Keystone at the Crossing, Indiana]." *Restaurant/Hotel Design International* (May 1988): vol. 10, no. 5, pp. 68–73.

Franks, Julia. "Best hotel over 300 rooms: Princeton Marriott, Plainsboro, New Jersey." *Restaurant/Hotel Design International* (October 1988): vol. 10, no. 10, pp. [50–53].

Fuller, Larry Paul. "Going Global/RTKL at 50: In Defiance of Stereotypes." *World Architecture* (January 1996): no. 42, pp. 24–65.

Gaskie, Margaret. "Patients first." *Architecture* (March 1993): vol. 82, no. 3, pp. 99–105.

Gantenbein, Douglas. "How not to design a park: Seattle settles on a Rouse project and awaits a new museum." *Architectural Record* (August 1987): vol. 175, no. 8, p. 63.

Geran, Monica. "Hotel Bellevue." *Interior Design* (October 1989): vol. 60, no.14, pp. [212–223].

"Growing in place: The Johns Hopkins Hospital, Baltimore, Maryland." *Architectural Record* (May 1984): vol. 172, no. 6, pp. 136–141.

Henderson, Justin. "RTKL's renovation of the Bank of Baltimore mixes the contemporary and the neoclassical." *Interiors* (April 1987): vol. 146, no. 9, pp. 194–197.

"IBM als Bauherr: seine Partnerschaft mit den Architekten." *Baumeister* (December 1988): vol. 85, no. 12, pp. 13–37.

Ivy Jr., Robert A. "A combination of audacity and skill: Northpark Mall, Miss: RTKL Associates Inc." *Architecture* (April 1986): vol. 75, no. 4, pp. 46–49, 108.

Jacob, Paul. "Urban oasis in Taiwan." *Urban Land* (December 1993): vol. 52, no. 12, pp. 9–10.

Johnson, Roger. "Harbour reborn." *Landscape Architecture* (August 1989): vol. 79, no. 6, pp. [36]–38.

Knight III, Carleton. "Clients: IBM returns to its roots: the latest phase in its off-and-on pursuit of architecture." *Architecture* (June 1986): vol. 75, no. 6, pp. [60]–73.

Kroloff, Reed. "Building Diplomacy." *Architecture* (January 1996): vol. 85., no. 1, pp. 115–117.

Leccese, Michael. "Brave old world: a new vision for suburban design." *Landscape Architecture* (December 1988): vol. 78, no. 8, pp. [56]–65.

Lufty, Carol. "Ambassador and Mrs. Walter Mondale in Japan." *Architectural Digest* (October 1995): vol. 52, no. 10, pp. [218]–[224], 232.

Mannion, Annemarie. "Matteson plan bridges the gap." *Inland Architect* (May–June 1990): vol. 34, no. 3, pp. 84–[88].

Mays, Vernon. "10,000 hotel rooms a year [Marriott Corporation]." *Progressive Architecture* (June 1988): vol. 69, no. 6, pp. 96–99.

McCracken, Laurin, ed. "RTKL: their international design." *Process Architecture* (July 1993): no. 111, entire issue (148 pp.).

McKee, Bradford. "Federal design/build: six projects reveal how the government has succeeded—and failed—by teaming architects and contractors." *Architecture* (October 1994): vol. 83, no. 10, pp. 109–115.

Miller, Robert L. "Dropped in on suburbia." *Landscape Architecture* (March 1992): vol. 82, no. 3, pp. 54–57.

Nesmith, Lynn. "RTKL Associates selected to design new town center for Reston." *Architecture* (February 1987): vol. 76, no. 2, pp. 12–13.

Newman, Morris. "ADA: the law of accommodation." *L.A. Architect* (January 1992): pp. 6–7.

"New design concept for Manhattan landmark [A & S Plaza]." *Urban Land* (January 1989): vol. 48, no. 1, p. 26.

"New York style comes to Chiba City." *Restaurant/Hotel Design International* (August 1989): vol. 11, no. 8, p. 16.

Olson, Christopher. "Renovated mall unearths a new image." *Building Design & Construction* (September 1989): vol. 30, no. 11, pp. [48–53].

"One Fountain Place, Cincinnati, Ohio." *Process Architecture* (November 1989): no. 86, pp. [82]–85.

Prowler, Donald. "Baltimore hits home with new baseball park." *Progressive Architecture* (June 1992): vol. 73, no. 6, p. 26.

Rath, Molly. "The Great Cultural Divide: Interoffice Diplomacy," *Washington Office* (March 1996): vol. 10, no. 9, pp. 17–35.

Rips, Bruce. "St. Louis Union Station and St. Louis Centre: the marketing of our architectural past." *Approach*, 1985, no. 3, pp. 2–5.

"RTKL Dallas's reach: buildings, projects, and plans." *Texas Architect* (November–December 1994): vol. 44, no. 6, pp. [38]–41.

"RTKL's Shanghai Plaza [Shanghai, China]," *Asian Architect and Contractor* (December 1995): vol. 25, no. 12, pp. 12, [14], 16.

Scharfe, Thomas. "Finding retail success in smaller markets." *Building Design & Construction* (March 1988): vol. 29, no. 3, pp. 56–61.

Schmertz, Mildred F. "Japanese imports." *Architecture* (September 1990): vol. 79, no. 9, pp. 72–[75], 154.

Shanley, Mary Kay. "Cultural crossbreed: Rivercenter, San Antonio, Texas." *Iowa Architect* (January–February 1989): vol. 37, no. 1, pp. 30–[31].

"Stratford Square, Bloomingdale, Illinois and White Marsh Mall, White Marsh, Maryland; architects: RTKL Associates." *Architectural Record* (April 1982): vol. 170, no. 5, pp. 126–133.

Sullivan, Ann. "New embassies open in Washington, D.C." *Architecture* (September 1994): vol. 83, no. 9, pp. 28–29.

Tilley, Ray Don. "Armoire's closet motif for retail design." *Texas Architect* (November–December 1991): vol. 41, no. 6, pp. 32–35.

"Tower City Center, Cleveland, Ohio. *Urban Land Institute. Project Reference File* (January–March 1994): pp. [1–4].

"The Federated Building, Cincinnati, Ohio, 1979." *Architectural Record* (April 1980): vol. 167, no. 4, pp. 126–129.

"Unbuilt awards [1990]." *Florida Architect* (November–December 1990): vol. 37, no. 6, pp. 10–21.

"Winners in the 1977 professional design competition of ASLA." *Landscape Architecture* (July 1977): vol. 67, no. 4, entire issue.

Yee, Roger. "Look to the Windows [Swedish Embassy]," *Contract Design* (February 1996): vol. 38, no. 2, pp. 64–67.

Yee, Roger. "Raze the Roof [Roosevelt Field Mall]," *Contract Design* (July 1994): vol. 36, no. 7.

Acknowledgments

Distilling 50 years of history—and all that goes with it—into a single volume is no small task. The full body of work, not to mention the enthusiasm and the talent of the people who created it, cannot possibly be captured by these pages. What we hope to have illustrated here, however, is that the enduring strength of RTKL is based in diversity, the dynamic of the team, and the spirit of co-operation.

With that, and on behalf of the Board of Directors, I would like to thank all the people who have been part of the RTKL team, most of whose names we have tried to include in this volume's end papers; our clients who, throughout our fifty years, trusted us to bring vision and integrity to their projects; the consultants and contractors we have worked with to make those projects a reality; and the friends of RTKL who have sung our praises in a variety of voices.

For the production of this book, we thank Thom McKay (RTKL, London) and Jo Helman (RTKL, Baltimore) for co-ordinating the effort and treading lightly through fifty years of history; the marketing staff in each office for assembling the information (Susan Ciccotti and Judy Staples in Baltimore, Ann Carper in Washington, Yvette Marentes in Dallas, Diana Cortes and Renata Tomko in Los Angeles); Larry Paul Fuller for his concise and comprehensive Introduction; and the Design Review Committee for their honest self-assessment of the work, the bulk of which found its way into the book.

We are also indebted to the talents of the many artists, model makers and photographers who have captured the portfolio, notably Marion E. Warren for much of the earlier work, the studio of Hedrich-Blessing, Maxwell MacKenzie and, of course, David Whitcomb.

Finally, we would like to thank IMAGES for the invitation to take part in this series and their unswerving guidance in shaping the book.

Harold L. Adams FAIA, RIBA, JIA

Credits for the Selected and Current Projects

A number on its own corresponds to the page on which the photographer's work is featured. Commonly, all pictures on the page belong to the same photographer, however, where several artists are featured on the same page, the corresponding image is listed in brackets by its caption number.

Joe Aker: 15 (a); 215 (1).
Richard Anderson: 206 (3); 225 (2).
Jaime Ardiles-Arce: 174; 175 (2–5) *Courtesy Architectural Digest © 1995 The Conde Nast Publications. All rights reserved. Used with permission.*
Art Associates (renderer): 225 (13).
John Barlow: 17 (a); 34 (1); 35 (3,4); 192 (c); 199 (c); 233 (34).
Art Beaulieu: 16 (c); 193 (a); 194 (b); 197 (c); 198 (c); 199 (a); 201 (c).
Bielenberg: 52 (1).
Blackmon/Winters: 92 (1,2).
J. Brough Schamp: 14 (a); 77 (4); 150 (1); 210 (3); 237 (9).
Burns Photography: 11 (e).
Charles Callister, Jr: 228 (6).
James Cant: 231 (23).
Thomas F. Cioffi (1940–1995): front cover painting.
Clique Production: 17 (b).
Len Curtis (renderer): 205 (10).
Paul Dino: 202 (b).
Ray Duee: 15 (c).
John Gillan: 32 (2); 33 (5).
Burt Glinn: 12 (f); 13 (b); 75 (3); 223 (1); 225 (1); 228 (4); 236 (3).
Tim Griffith/The Images Publishing Group: 40 (1); 41 (2–4); 53 (1); 156 (1); 157 (2,4); 233 (31).
Steve Hall/Hedrich-Blessing: back cover; 12 (e); 173; 178 (2); 179 (4); 235 (3).
Satashi Hasakawa: 114 (2); 115 (3–6); 208 (12).
Hedrich-Blessing: 13 (e); 63 (5); 120 (1); 169 (2); 203 (7); 206 (4,5); 207 (7–10); 208 (13); 213 (3); 214 (9); 215 (2–6); 219 (4,5,7,8,9); 220 (10,14); 230 (15,17); 235 (4).
Jim Hedrich/Hedrich-Blessing: 15 (b,d); 138 (1).
Peter Howard: 186.
Masayaso Ikeda: 208 (14).
Steve Jost: 195 (b); 201 (a).
Erich Ansel Koyama: 26 (1).
Kudo Photo: 225 (11).
Nathaniel Lieberman: 206 (6).
Fred Light: 129 (3,4); 235 (6).
Breton Littlehales: 16 (d); 191 (a,c); 192 (a,b); 193 (b,c); 194 (c); 195 (a,c); 196 (a,b,c); 198 (a); 199 (b); 201 (b).
Victoria Lefcourt: 100 (1); 101 (2–5); 213 (1).
Scott McDonald/Hedrich-Blessing: 14 (e); 15 (e); 16 (a); 23; 24 (1); 25 (4); 27 (1); 29 (1,4); 44 (1); 45 (2); 46 (2); 47 (3); 50 (1); 51 (2–4); 64 (2); 65 (3); 66 (5–7); 67 (8); 70 (2); 71 (3–5); 93 (1,2); 94 (1,2); 96 (1,2): 97 (1,2); 99 (1,2); 103; 104 (1); 105 (3–5); 116 (1); 117 (2–4); 119 (2–5); 120

(1); 121 (4,5); 137; 152 (1); 153 (2,4); 180 (2); 181 (3,5); 182 (6); 183 (7–9); 209 (17); 214 (8); 216 (7); 220 (13); 221 (17); 223 (5); 224 (10); 226 (5); 232 (26); 233 (33, 35).
E Alan McGee: 139 (2).
Maxwell MacKenzie: 14 (b); 56 (2); 57 (4); 60 (2); 61 (3,5); 95 (1,2); 98 (1,2); 150 (2); 151 (3–5); 164 (2); 165 (6); 166 (2,3); 168 (1); 169 (3,4); 170 (2); 171 (3,4); 177 (2); 208 (11); 209 (1); 210 (4–6); 211 (7–9); 213 (2,4,5); 214 (6,7,10); 220 (11,12,16); 221 (20); 223 (2,4); 224 (8); 230 (19); 231 (21).
Jon Miller/Hedrich-Blessing: 108 (1); 109 (2–4); 118 (1–5).
Joseph W Molitor Photography: 11 (a,b); 12 (a,c); 203 (2,3); 219 (2).
Nagase: 178 (3).
Mary E. Nichols: 110 (2); 111 (3–5).
Tony Nathan: 200 (a).
Dennis O'Kain: 222 (21).
J Parker: 230 (14).
Erhard Pfeiffer: 128 (2); 129 (5); 204 (1).
Photogenics: 205 (7).
Lautman Photography: 223 (3).
Janice Rettaliata: 77 (3); 204 (3).
Rion Rizzo/Creative Sources: 228 (5).
Mark Segal: 57 (3).
Bob Shimer/Hedrich-Blessing: 13 (c); 14 (c); 48 (1); 49 (2,3); 74 (2); 139 (1); 229 (10).
Ron Solomon: 47 (5); 219 (6); 235 (1).
Robert Stahman: 13 (d).
Fred Stocker: 128 (1).
Wes Thompson: 222 (22); 229 (13).
Peter Vanderwalker: 112 (2); 113 (3,4); 209 (16).
Adrian Velcescu/Av Media: 159 (3).
Jay Venezia: 26 (2); 191 (b); 194 (a); 197 (a); 198 (b); 200 (b); 232 (27).
M E Warren: 10 (b,c,d,e); 11 (a); 12 (d); 14 (d); 203 (1,6).
Ron Watts: 229 (8).
David Whitcomb: 11 (f); 12 (b); 13 (a); 16 (b); 25 (3,5,6); 27 (2); 29 (2,3); 30 (1); 31 (2–4); 33 (3,4); 42 (1); 43 (2–4); 45 (3,4); 47 (4); 52 (2); 57 (5); 61 (4); 75 (1); 89 (2,3); 126 (1,2);127 (3–7); 132 (1,2) *Used by permission from Disney Enterprises, Inc.*; 133 (3–7) *Used by permission from Disney Enterprises, Inc.*; 134 (2); 135 (3–7); 138 (2); 148 (2); 149 (3); 165 (3–5); 200 (c); 203 (3); 204 (2,4); 205 (8); 206 (1); 212 (11–13); 216 (8,9); 219 (1); 220 (16); 221 (18,19); 224 (7); 225 (12); 228 (1,2,3,7); 229 (9,11,12); 230 (16,18); 231 (22,24); 232 (25,28,29); 233 (30); 235 (2).
A Zake: 16 (e).

Index

Bold page numbers refer to projects
included in Selected and Current Works